How to Be Less Miserable

How to Be Less Miserable

End the Negative Mind Loops and Find Joy

Lybi Ma

BLACK STONE PUBLISHING

Published in 2025 by Blackstone Publishing
Cover and book design by Alenka Vdovič Linaschke
Illustrations by Hamil Ma

Some names and identifying details have been changed to protect the privacy of individuals.

Printed in the United States of America

First edition: 2025
ISBN 979-8-212-61597-6
Self-Help / Emotions

Version 1

Blackstone Publishing
31 Mistletoe Rd.
Ashland, OR 97520

www.BlackstonePublishing.com

To my big, beautiful family in order of height—
Chelsea, Jessie, Elizabeth, Monica, Luise, Carl,
Mark, KC, Matthew, Zak, David, and Amiel
(depending on heels, inserts, and proper sleep)

Contents

Introduction

It takes an open mind to manage the uncertainties and negatives we encounter in life. We like the ground we stand on to be predictable and solid, but then unsettling things like the COVID pandemic occur, proving that we often don't know what will happen. There are unknowns of all kinds—job loss, natural disasters, catastrophic illnesses, sudden death, and so much more. Any number of things can render us without food, shelter, or security. No one escapes not knowing, especially now.

The pandemic influenced the rates of loneliness, depression, and anxiety, pushing people inside their heads. According to the World Health Organization, the global prevalence of anxiety and depression has increased by 25 percent in the last few years. Our negative mental loops cycle on replay and still do. In daily interactions with family, friends, and colleagues, I saw that some people were more equipped to manage the negative thinking the brain wants us to suffer. These people soldiered on, leading healthy lives, while others did not fare as well. I wanted to find out why. What does it take to bypass the brain's tendency for suffering?

I have worked at *Psychology Today* magazine for nearly twenty-five years. The publication, founded in 1967, focuses on behavioral science, and its mission is to bring psychology research and literature to the general public. It also focuses on helping people manage their health and overall well-being. While it is not a peer-reviewed science journal, we work with contributors who have academic expertise in psychology and its related fields.

The publication's website and blog platform hosts more than nine hundred book authors, academic researchers, and journalists. It is the largest online behavioral science site in the world, featuring psychology lions such as the late Stanford existential psychiatrist Irvin Yalom, the late Nobel laureate Daniel Kahneman of Princeton, and Harvard's William Haseltine, who is known for his groundbreaking work on HIV/AIDS, among many others.

These researchers and mental health practitioners are in the trenches of new findings and clinical cases. I have learned a lot from them and wanted to share what I have discovered. My collaboration with them has given me the foundation and knowledge to write this book.

On a personal level, I have also fought with negative loops inside my head and have managed to—mostly—win the war. When I was younger, I used to overgeneralize and draw bleak conclusions about things that happened or were about to happen. I often thought the worst about things and that the worst would be forever. I thought I knew when someone wanted to *hate me until I died*. I personalized *everything* and blamed myself for *everything*, even when it was not my fault. Here are some of the ways I encouraged my negativity:

- Catastrophizing: "I know the worst will happen to me, even though the evidence points to the contrary."
- All-or-Nothing Thinking: "My error, however small, equals abject failure. There is no middle ground because everything is black and white."
- Overgeneralization: "I am an *absolute* loser."
- Filtering: "I focus on everything negative. I don't see anything positive."
- Mind Reading: "I know that whatever you are thinking about me is bad and critical."
- Personalization: "I blame myself for everything, even when I know it is not my fault."
- Emotional Reasoning: "I feel like I'm a fraud; therefore, I am one. My feelings are reality."
- Shoulda, Woulda, Coulda: "I should have known. My actions always lead to terrible outcomes."

Perhaps you can relate to this kind of thought process. Most of us can.

I learned how to disengage from negativity, but it took time through reading, meditating, and changing my way of thinking. A big "aha" moment for me was taking up yoga, something I have now been practicing for decades. Some people think that this form of exercise has become too trite and mainstream, but the truth is that it works. Yoga lowers stress, reduces anxiety, and improves mood. Most of all, it quiets my mind. This daily practice helped change my fruitless habit of negativity. Now, I try to be more self-aware, compassionate, and open. I also count my blessings and focus more on others than myself. I sit in nature, listen to my body, connect with others, know what I value, and try not to fight with life.

In this book, I will examine different aspects of negative thinking, from why we do it to why it's so hard to stop doing it, as well as methods that challenge negativity and replace it with a more positive mindset. Most people engage in negative thinking to some degree or another. The strategies discussed in these pages—based, in large part, on information from scholars and researchers I have worked with—can help us manage and overcome it.

In the following chapters, we will look at:

- How the mind is programmed to work against us (when we realize this, we will solve a lot of our problems).
- Why life can be disappointing and unhappy.
- Why we thwart ourselves and how this prevents us from moving forward.
- The truth about hard emotions and how to embrace them.
- How knowing who we are can lead to self-agency and less misery.
- How to be open to life and opportunity.
- Why we need to apply kindness and compassion.
- Why our connections with others keep us going.
- How to live in the present moment.
- How to view happiness realistically.
- And knowing what we value is key.

This book is based on neuroscience research and how we can use this science to help us take control of our minds—even though the mind automatically prefers to indulge in unfavorable and catastrophic thinking. The mind wants to protect us from unknown uncertainties, but it does too good a job sometimes, and this results in our daily lives being hijacked by unhappy thoughts. Our minds end up throwing us off, and we become distressed over the past and get worked up about the future, locking ourselves in mental pain. In truth, our thoughts are just thoughts, and not much more. Today is what matters, not yesterday, not tomorrow.

This book is also informed by my background. My family is Hui from the Qinghai–Tibet Plateau in Northwest China. The Hui people are Muslims, and they can be found in small numbers all around the world—in Thailand, Kyrgyzstan, Malaysia, Saudi Arabia, and North America, among many other regions. The Mainland Chinese Hui, however, number more than ten million and are the country's fourth largest ethnic group. I have hundreds of cousins who live in the hometown where my parents were born and raised.

My parents came from a time of mule carts, cotton-quilted shoes, sheepskin jackets, men in braids, and palanquins—covered boxes that required up to six men to carry them, depending on the extravagance. Marriages were arranged, and firstborn sons took over the business of a family household. They had a different worldview.

My mother, for one, would sit in the kitchen while the rain clattered on the roof and then say, "Heart narrow," which was her way of commenting that the weather made her feel down. But rather than basking in it, she'd get up to make supper. Duty called. And my dad regularly stopped to contemplate life. He would lie down in the driveway looking at the stars, in awe of the expansiveness of space, knowing that the universe was filled with wonder and how we were insignificant in comparison. Mom would shout at him to get up off the driveway, "What if you fall asleep?" "You'll wake me," he'd say.

I think Mom was alert to the dangers in life while Dad was more a man of science. And neuroscience shows how humans are inherently attentive to all things negative, things that make us feel worried, anxious, and disagreeable, among many other distressing behaviors. Our filters are alert to the treacherous and hard things in life. Fortunately, Dad had some wherewithal to be open to life's wonder. And fortunately, Mom was vigilant about keeping us safe.

My older siblings shared our parents' predispositions. My older sister was alert, like Mom, to uncertainty and peril; my brothers, like Dad, embraced wonder. They also, like my parents, had concerns about losing our Hui identity by becoming too American.

Like my siblings, I am a product of two cultures, and because of this, I often have different reactions to situations in life. I realize that Western culture does sometimes feed the "monkey mind," where the inner voice worries and churns, but Western culture also encourages positive cultural aspirations like personal freedom and individual expression. In turn, Eastern thought promotes important aspects of living, such as harmony with others and detachment from desires that may make us miserable.

I am taking the best of the two worlds that have shaped who I am, and I am sharing that here. In doing so, I'm hoping to address why we suffer from constant negativity and how to find ways out of that mindset. Hopefully, we can all be a little "less miserable" as a result.

Chapter One

We Are Miserable by Default

My neighbor once told me that he often dresses, ties his shoelaces, drags his toothbrush around, starts the car, drives down the parkway, and arrives at his office without much mental effort and that this sometimes alarms him. Yet we all do it. We all have days where we go through the motions like an automaton. How many mornings have I walked to the train station without noticing who I passed along the way?

For this zombie-like state, we can thank the "default mode network," which is located in the brain's prefrontal, parietal, and temporal lobes. The theory of the default mode was first studied in the late 1990s and early 2000s by researchers, including Marcus Raichle and Gordon Shepherd, both from the Washington University School of Medicine and authors of *Angelo Mosso's Circulation of Blood in the Human Brain*. They found that these brain regions activate when we are not engaged in any specific cognitive task in order to prevent mental overload and allow our minds to wander.

The Default Mode Network

This default mode protects us from applying brainpower where it isn't needed. We simply switch off and go on autopilot. Mundane chores, like sweeping the floor, benefit from this kind of auto-effort, in which the body does all the work and saves the mind from taxing itself. This is also partly because heuristics are at work—these are mental shortcuts that let us make decisions, judgment calls, and problem-solve swiftly. The brain doesn't want to expend too much mental effort on certain routine tasks, so it uses shortcuts to approach problems quickly. For example, financial professionals use heuristics to quickly analyze data and decide what investments to make. If the earnings of a company's share go below a certain number, then financial advisers may recommend that we buy that company's stock *now*.

Many researchers have studied heuristics, but a few people to note are the late Princeton professor of psychology and Nobel laureate Daniel Kahneman, and his late collaborator, cognitive and mathematical psychologist Amos Tversky of Stanford. They found that people make hasty judgments when they are uncertain about something.

Aside from mental shortcuts, the brain is wired to complete tasks like breathing, walking, washing dishes, or sweeping the floor without thought or conscious awareness. On the flip side, more advanced mechanical tasks, such as building a house, require thought and conscious awareness. This makes logical sense, as we don't want to be thinking about every muscle as we move about our day. If we are focused on every movement—for example, while riding a bicycle—we might tumble. Letting muscle memory do its job is a useful thing.

However, letting our autopilot have free rein where it has no business can be dangerous. The task of driving a car is a good example. A study published in *The Journal of the Human Factors and Ergonomics Society* showed how the mind wanders while driving. I don't need a science journal to tell me this. I often zone out at the wheel, especially when I get closer to home—and this is how accidents happen. Frankly, knowing the roads by rote isn't always a good thing.

Our autopilot even switches on in the middle of conversations. Our heads may continue to nod, even though the words conveyed by the person speaking to us don't register.

This default mode network also stores daydreams, fantasies, and nostalgia, which can be positive and even creative. Unfortunately, it stores ruminations of past disturbances and future imaginings as well. Unsurprisingly, this is related to various disorders, including Alzheimer's and Parkinson's, in which the mind loses its hold on reality. Another factor is the default mode network's relation to hyperconnectivity in the brain, whereby too many connections are made between neurons. This is something associated with conditions including epileptic seizures and even schizophrenia.

The default mode network is also a friend to anxiety, worry, and pessimism. Negative thinking and critical self-talk operate on such an automatic system. It promotes the noise inside our heads. Sometimes, it gets so noisy that it spirals in a perpetual loop, which can drive anyone out of their mind. When the inner critic barges in and makes its appearance, the pessimistic thought then proceeds to flood the mind on a repetitive track of involuntary replay. Negativity takes hold in perpetuity.

The Neverending Mental Loop

It's human nature to think about how we do not measure up, the reasons why we are behind in life, how we could be better parents, why our partners are annoyed with us, or why we are annoyed with ourselves. We wind up rolling around in our thoughts, finding ourselves in limitless unease.

When we're on this negative track, we're not open to growth and progress. We are stuck in a distressed frame of mind that is often absolute, which is a very terrible cognitive distortion that the mind likes to pull. The person who suffers from this kind of polarized thinking uses words like *never, forever, always,* and *nothing*—"I'll never amount to anything." "I will be a loser forever." "I will always be alone."

Here's a simple example. I spent an hour reading on a city park bench surrounded by sunshine, flowers, and a pleasant ambiance, but what will I remember most? The rat that ran on the brick edge of the garden path. I know rats are everywhere here, but now I will *never* go back to that park.

Many researchers have examined what they call the "negativity bias," including University of Pennsylvania psychologists Paul Rozin and Edward Royzman, who wrote the important and well-cited study in the *Personality and Social Psychology Review* journal. Essentially, they concluded, we focus on the negative, from distressing thoughts, anxious worries, and unhappy emotions to traumatic events and disagreeable interactions. We are inclined to look at events, in the past and future, through this filter. This built-in tendency is a byproduct of our evolution as a species. Our hunter-gatherer ancestors had to be alert and ready because a predator could be around any corner. It was more important to avoid being eaten than to find food.

For early humans, this was a key feature of the brain as the brain wants us to survive. Different body parts—like the eyes and the nose—send information to the brain, and impending danger activates the amygdala, which is located in the temporal lobes above the ear. This is where emotions like fear and anger are processed. The amygdala is responsible for the flight-and-fight response, where we either settle in to fight or flee. If I smell gas, I had better look for the source; otherwise, the house might explode.

Evolution nurtures the feeling that something awful is about to happen. The human brain hasn't changed that much since the dawn of man. We continue to operate by these rules and have a thought bias toward the negative because the brain is trying to be protectively error-prone—that is, the brain makes errors in judgment to protect us. There is good reason for this. In the modern era, we may not know if a stranger is trustworthy; therefore, the brain must make an automatic choice. This is why we might gloss over someone who seems to be good and decent and, instead, zero in on someone who seems harmful. *Should I trust or not trust this person?* We put ourselves in danger when we misjudge a bad person. Being alert to such negatives keeps us alive; this is evolution at work.

Because we are wired to look for danger, we also tend to look for danger in the wrong places. We are loss- and risk-averse. We remember losing money more than we remember winning or finding money. We remember painful things, and we forget pleasant things. The work of Robert Sapolsky can help us parse this. He is a professor of biology and neurology at Stanford University and the author of many books including *Why Zebras Don't Get Ulcers*. Humans and primates have a more activated stress response than other animals. Even if there's no danger, humans remember the stress of previous danger and anticipate future similar events to happen again and again. This can cause mood disorders and other illnesses. Meanwhile, animals return to a calm state—the cheetah chases the zebra; then the zebra placidly returns to the savanna to graze. Humans don't do that.

Roy Baumeister, likely one of the most cited social scientists of our time, has thought deeply about human nature and the pull toward the negatives of life. We peg our minds to the bad things that happen more than the positive or the neutral. He found this propensity in all areas of life, from bad relationships, unhappy workplaces, and terrible sex to poor parenting and horrible memories. Baumeister found that negative emotions are more important to us than positive ones. He summarizes the idea with the catchphrase, "Bad is stronger than good." Humans spend much more time avoiding bad moods rather than creating or prolonging good moods, he found.

The human mind wanders to the negatives of the past and future all the time. Everyone does this, but some of us do it more than others. Mostly it's about things that happened or might happen, and things that didn't or won't sit well with us. The mind is, then, set on a brooding track and remains there.

We also focus on how things will eventually pan out one day somewhere in the distant future. We fantasize and dream of what tomorrow will bring. I used to do that myself in my youth. I dreamed of a flawless home, an exciting career, an adoring husband, and a flock of superb children. Many of these things did pan out. I do have superb children, of course, with all the lumps and bumps they are supposed to have. I do have an adoring husband. I do have meaningful work, though I am not the exciting superagent spy I thought I might have been.

We Have a Tendency to Fixate on the Terrible

In a study published in the *Journal of Personality and Social Psychology* in 1998, subjects were shown a variety of photographs—positive images like people riding a roller-coaster, neutral images like a hairdryer, and negative images like a gun pointed at the camera. The researchers found that the brains of the subjects lit up more when viewing the image of the gun.

The brain is prejudiced toward the negative, and according to psychologists Rozin, Royzman, and other researchers, this can be described in a few ways.

- *First, we recall the bad.* When we have two memories that are equal in emotional weight, for example, we tend to remember the unpleasant one more potently.
- *Second, our dread increases over time.* We may feel somewhat anxious about an upcoming event, such as a medical procedure. Yet as the date approaches, we become more and more distressed over time.
- *Third, we remember our mistakes the most.* We just gave a presentation, and our colleagues applauded our brilliant ideas, but we made one small mistake with a calculation, and that's what we recall.
- *Fourth, we think repeatedly about negative events.* Negativity is more complex than positivity, and we have to work to wrap our minds around it. Essentially, we

> are wired to fixate on negative threats so that we can thwart those threats.

Adverse interactions with other people and general malaise like to stick in our heads. Why do media outlets splash negative headlines? Because we are more attentive and drawn to bad news—this means their ratings go up and they generate more advertising revenue. We need to pay attention to survive. The media gives the brain what it wants to pay attention to.

The tendency toward negative thinking can also harm our relationships. At first impression, for example, we may focus on the minor flaws of a new person we meet. This is a form of *stranger danger.* We may even focus on the negative in long-term relationships by immediately feeling defensive when we hear an inkling of criticism.

Of course, sometimes people show us who they really are the first time we meet them. Maya Angelou wrote, "When someone shows you who they are, believe them the first time." Depending on the situation, whether at a cocktail party or on a city street, it may require being cautious when meeting someone new.

The Myth of the Pursuit of Happiness

The human tendency toward negative thinking is a survival strategy baked into our makeup. For that reason, it makes perfect sense to fight this predisposition. That is why we find ourselves seeking extreme positivity. We want to be happy.

When we search the word "happy" on Amazon, we will find book titles like *Happy Healthy*, *The How of Happiness*, *The Path to Happiness*, or just plain *Happy*. Many of us believe that being happy is our absolute birthright because of the

American Constitution, which states, "We hold these truths to be self-evident, that all men are created equal, that they are endowed by their Creator with certain unalienable Rights, that among these are Life, Liberty and the pursuit of Happiness."

We are taught to seek extreme positivity. Yet 29 percent of Americans have reported feeling depressed at some point in life, while other cultures—for example, in Asia and parts of Europe, among other regions—suffer at much lower rates. Are Americans working too hard to find bliss?

The emotional cost of chasing happiness is, perhaps, too high. Ironically, chasing happiness doesn't generally make us happy. It's probably wiser to take a more tempered approach that no one emotion should trump any of the others, such as anger, sadness, or calmness, just to name a few.

The so-called "bucket list" is the ultimate example of this hot pursuit of happiness. If we can cross off enough items from the list, we will supposedly achieve the good life. Some of these items may be grand, like setting foot in the ancient city of Petra. Others may be awe-filled, such as looking up at the Northern Lights. Still others may be quirky, like baking bread in the active geothermal areas of Iceland.

People who take their bucket lists seriously put an emotional premium on these must-do events; they believe these activities are supposed to help them reach a certain happiness quotient. But neuroscience tells another story: Chasing this list does not create lasting contentment. Depending on the individual, we each have a set point of happiness. Over time, our ecstatic highs naturally come down, and our desperate lows come back up all on their own as we move back to our normal mood level. Many researchers have examined and refined this set point, most notably psychologist Sonja Lyubomirsky, author of *The How of Happiness* and professor at the University of California, Riverside. She and her colleagues showed that our happiness set point is encoded in our genes. Some of us are just born happier.

The set-point theory is also related to the work of the late Philip Brickman of the University of Michigan and the late Donald Campbell of Lehigh University, authors of the influential paper "Hedonic Relativism and Planning the Good Society." They researched the idea of the "hedonic treadmill," or hedonic adaptation, where humans return to their stable level of emotions, no matter what positive or negative event happens to take place. More money, for example, does not mean more happiness.

Extreme elation and extreme misery don't last. We each land at the set point of happiness we're accustomed to. No matter how awe-inspiring, the glow after a fabulous occasion will always fade. In other words, try as we might, we will not keep Italian tenor Andrea Bocelli performing an aria in the forefront of our minds as time passes.

Pursuing our bucket list items may not bring happiness because the focus is sometimes on what we don't have, and our expectations of what we think will make us happy do not last. We might instead pursue well-being and a meaningful life.

What to Put on a *Real* Bucket List

If we *must* have a bucket list, Glenn Geher, an evolutionary psychologist at the State University of New York at New Paltz, has a sensible idea of what we should include on such a tally. He contends that we should think about what matters, not so much about novel quests like swimming with dolphins and spending thousands of dollars on a coveted Super Bowl seat.

For Geher, it all has to do with staying connected with others, as well as doing one's part in making the world a better place. He knows that broken bonds and estrangements can have lasting ill effects and that people who have suffered a high number of estrangements during their lifetime are more anxious than others who are safely within their tribes. For our ancestors, being outcast into the jaws of wild animals meant certain death, and as a result, evolution has incentivized our brains to stay on the good side of others within our groups. This ancient survival need has stayed with us; therefore, learning how to make amends can help ensure a person survives.

People are cooperative by nature. When young children see a person in distress, empathy kicks in, making them more likely to come to the person's aid. This innate need to help others is smart behavior, as this also ensures the helper's place within their tribe. Plus, the benevolent person enjoys the reciprocity of kindness and goodwill. Benevolence and helping others are part of caring for the world and the people in it. The planet's future depends on compassion.

A trip to marvel at the glaciers in Patagonia sounds great, but these quests will not bring lasting fulfillment. Just living, day in and day out, and knowing that staying connected, doing good for others, as well as not picking a fight with life, can be a path to reach fulfillment.

Sometimes We Think Too Much

Often, we have a habit of thinking too much in a negative pattern. An elderly friend of mine demonstrated this particularly well. She was often wise about politics and modern-day living, and I found her insights in these areas useful. But as wise as she was, she had a lifelong fixation on an unfortunate relationship with her mother-in-law. "My mother-in-law was so mean to me. She was always picking on me," this friend often told me. The mother-in-law had criticized my friend's every effort—her cooking, parenting, how she managed her household, what her child ate, who she socialized with, and even what my friend wore. The mother-in-law had been dead for many years, and I encouraged her to let this memory go, but the mother-in-law's criticisms were stuck in my friend's mind. This was unfortunate, as it appeared to hold her back from the joy of a full life. She said that she felt unhappy and unfulfilled most of the time. I don't know what other problems bothered her, but she mentioned her mother-in-law with great regularity.

For many of us, thinking too much can be a permanent pastime, as well as a hallmark of angst. Let's face it, we worry and ruminate, and some of us do this *a lot.* The term *navel-gazing* is derived from the Greek word *omphaloskepsis* (*omphalos* for navel and *skepsis* for speculation). *Omphaloskepsis* was originally the contemplation of the navel as an aid to meditation. The Hindi deployed the same type of practice with the focal point being the chakra. Like the Greek monks, the Hindi contemplated the meaning of life, as well as existence. It was introspection and existential thought at a higher level. This type of reflection and meditation is supposed to bring us to nirvana, but it often doesn't because people may turn to harmful ruminating, rather than helpful meditating.

The term "navel-gazing" has since become synonymous with roiling in one's feelings and thoughts in a self-absorbed way—in short, ruminating. It is now considered an indulgence with no concern for others whatsoever. In this sense, navel-gazing is not the meditative state it is supposed to be; it is the exact opposite of reflection and meditation. In the modern day, it is akin to wallowing inside one's head. Essentially, because of our evolutionary programming, we sometimes become stuck in a loop of gazing at our navels.

Numerous researchers, including the late Susan Nolen-Hoeksema, who was a professor of psychology at Yale University and the author of *Women Who Think Too Much*, showed the detriments of overthinking. Reflection slides on a continuum, from healthy contemplation to unhealthy rumination, and ruminative thought feeds a continual mind loop. Nolen-Hoeksema found this to be a hallmark of depression and anxiety. Her interest in women's moods extended from data that they suffer higher rates of mood disorders than men. In addition, she found that women are more vulnerable to depressive symptoms than men.

Rumination Is a Loop of Angst

As a child, if I sat around feeling sorry for myself, my mother would gently rap her knuckles on the top of my head and admonish me. "So selfish," she would say. "Go clean toilet." To Mom, who was born and raised in the Qinghai–Tibet Plateau of China, a person should not nurture neurotic thinking or dwell on the tiny things that are wrong in life. This would allow catastrophizing and overgeneralizing to take control.

I would not admit it back then, but my mother was right. Ruminating over petty grievances isn't at all helpful. (Ruminating, however, is not the same as thinking about an event that needs processing—for example, grieving over the death of a beloved dog needs time and deliberation.) Extended cogitating over minor gripes can lead to negativity and mood disorders.

Certainly, bad things do happen—say, a death in the family or losing a job—but that doesn't mean we need to fall into a negative cycle of self-talk set on phrases such as, "I am so terrible I lost that job. I am a failure."

Psychologist Albert Ellis, the father of Rational Emotive Behavior Therapy and the author of books including *How to Control Your Anxiety*, coined the term "awfulizing"—when we think a scenario or situation is 100 percent worse than it really is. Learning how to regulate our emotions is key to combating this sort of pessimistic outlook.

Ethan Kross, a professor of psychology at the University of Michigan, as well as the director of the university's Emotion and Self Control Lab, has done all sorts of studies on distancing oneself from the self, a useful technique that may promote healthy self-regulation. He found that we can distance ourselves from negative thinking by referring to ourselves in the third person. Third-person thinking is a rhetorical device called "illeism." It helps us distance ourselves from negative thoughts, and it can help regulate our emotions toward more even-keeled reflection. We can act like a fly on the wall in the movie called *My Life*, and sometimes we watch ourselves mope in misery: *Jane is feeling sorry for herself because she didn't get that party invitation.*

This third-person perspective lets us observe a situation from afar. The first time I heard an aunt speak in the third person, I had to stop and listen. She said, "The shop clerk was not kind to Auntie Lin." My aunt addressed herself by her first name, and she had a funny knowing smile on her face like she knew she didn't have to buy into the negativity—her own or anyone else's. I learned a lot by watching and listening to this wise aunt.

Observe the Suffering

Many of us do not focus on the self in the ways that we should, as in self-care; instead, we focus on the self through negative deliberation that can actually shorten our lives. A paper in the journal *Neurobiology of Aging* published in 2021 shows that highly anxious and worried older adults had brains with much less gray matter. Essentially, anxiety can lead to shorter telomeres—structures made from DNA sequences and proteins found at the end of chromosomes. Telomeres shorten when cells divide. In effect, they get shorter as we age. When telomeres are too short, they cannot divide, which means cell death and a sure sign of accelerated aging. This reduces longevity, impairs stem cell and tissue function, and increases heart and infectious diseases.

Life does seem disappointing at times, regardless of negative deliberations, especially if we think we will only be happy if we're with that one certain person, have a particular job title, or own a specific house with a white picket fence. We may think that achieving that one-and-only thing is part and parcel of personal glory. "But disappointment resides somewhere between expectations and reality," said Tara Well, a professor of psychology at Barnard College, Columbia University and the author of *Mirror Meditation: The Power of Neuroscience and Self-Reflection*. There are various ways we fall into the trap of feeling discontent. Well argues that having very specific expectations sets us up for grave disappointment because it's hard for us to get everything we want and desire.

The expectation of life to be 100 percent amazing can lead to discontent. Researchers have explored a person's level of happiness, intelligence, and pleasure, among other items.

They wanted to, for example, find out how happy or intelligent a person would want to be. People prefer to be about 70 to 80 percent happy or intelligent, but not 100 percent, according to research in the journal *Psychological Science*. This idea of *just enough* happiness or intelligence was even more apparent in other cultures, such as Japan and India. People from these cultures preferred a level of happiness that was about 9 percent lower than nations like the United States or the United Kingdom.

Good Enough Is Good

Having a group-oriented nature makes people more likely to be satisfied at an 80 percent level of happiness. Their wider perspective may lead them to feel *just enough* happiness and not more than they *need* to be. This idea of just enough is in line with adopting a good enough life.

Things that can help us find contentment in being good enough:

- Find out what you are good at.
- Usually, it is something that you enjoy doing.
- And this is important: think about the *process*, not so much the *results*.
- It's even better when you remember what has meaning and value to *you*.
- Put aside what others say you should do.

Perhaps this is because Eastern cultures are typically collectivist, and Western cultures are typically individualistic. Collectivism stresses the importance of the community, while individualism stresses the importance of the individual. A good way to understand the difference is to imagine how a person might view a painting. An individualist might focus on an object in the foreground, while the collectivist might view the painting as a whole. According to research published in the *Personality and Social Psychology Bulletin*, Westerners see *parts* and Easterners see *wholes*. While looking at an aquarium, Easterners are more likely to see background elements like seaweed or a group of fish, while Westerners are more likely to notice the biggest fish.

Lawrence White, a professor of psychology at Beloit College in Wisconsin and author of the book *Culture Conscious: Briefings on Culture, Cognition, and Behavior*, studies human behavior in various corners of the world. He finds holistic thinking is more prevalent in cultures that practice Confucian, Buddhist, or Hindu traditions. In holistic philosophy, dark meets light, hot meets cold, and opposites coexist. In terms of happiness, holistic thinking adds a dose of sadness, which makes both emotions feel whole and complete.

Researchers like White advance the idea that all cultures can learn from each other. Learning from people of different places will open us. This approachable view may help us with our mental spirals and ruts. When we do that, we may find the passion for the things that matter—positive engagement in relationships, work, and life as a whole. We can tap into the cognitive skills that will help move us beyond the negativity that holds us back.

We want a happy life, and we pursue this with a lot of effort, yet we fixate on what is bleak and terrible. This compulsion toward a negative mindset can be perpetual, and it takes a toll on our mental and physical well-being. A person's criticisms, gloomy perspectives, and general pessimism wire the brain to promote feelings of anger and anxiety, among other difficult mental states. The stress of negativity is also detrimental to physical health; it raises blood pressure, weakens the immune system, and decreases the capacity to combat inflammation and illness.

However, we can move away from this misery by being aware of and regulating our emotions—hard ones like fear, jealousy, disappointment, and others. This healthy management helps us deal with life's ambiguities, combat all-or-nothing thinking, do away with hard feelings like shame and guilt, and defy self-sabotage to live a life free of distress.

Chapter Two

How to Handle the Ambiguity of Life

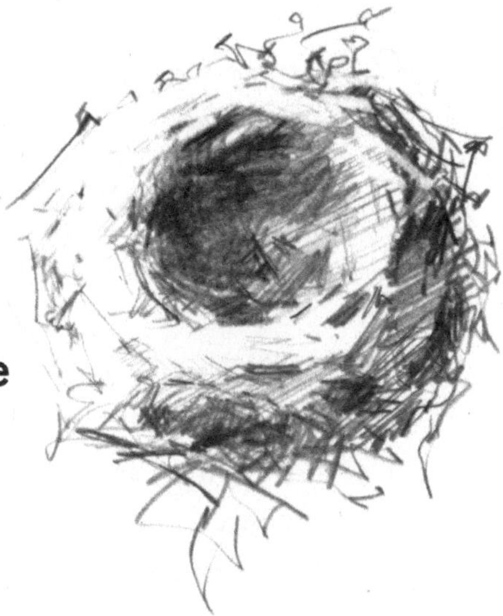

We like the predictable, and we want solid ground to stand on, but life is ambiguous and often unforeseeable. We don't know what will happen from one day to the next.

I had a friend who worried about a lot of things, but she shared with me her uncertainties about relationships the most. "Will I ever meet someone?" "Will I be alone forever?" "Will I have kids without a partner?" "Will I make enough money to do that?" These kinds of uncertainties alarmed her. I tried to be as encouraging as I could, but no one could answer these questions with total certainty. The best I could do was listen. People are grateful when we hear what they have to say.

We know a good life comes with imperfections, but we can still be thrown off by ambiguity. It is difficult to manage uncertainty when life is forever hurling unforeseeable surprises at us, especially in the last few years with the pandemic, war, inflation, and continued political upheaval.

I lost my job and have no clue how I'll feed my family.

A 7.4 magnitude earthquake destroyed my home.

A catastrophic illness has befallen a family member, and I am at a loss.

My partner left me without warning, took his belongings, and fled.

My child is heading to college. Now what?

Many things can change in life, and this can push us into a loop of distress. If we are not firmly standing on our own two feet, uncertainty can take us for a spin. Some people turn to the absolute certainty of extreme religiosity; some prefer conspiracy theories, while others depend on tarot cards and signs. However, no one escapes ambiguity.

The brain does prefer simple cut-and-dried situations. It uses mental shortcuts like heuristics to conserve our cognitive efforts—for example, we make quick decisions based on previous experiences. Essentially, the brain likes to simplify its thinking and avoid the difficulties of having mixed feelings. The mind's inclination toward clarity and simplicity can make it hard on us whenever we're dealing with any type of ambiguity. In general, humans have a negative bias when faced with unknowns; this bias can be fed by others who shout that doomsday is coming, which feels possible when there's an earthquake, followed by an eclipse, a bridge collapse, freak weather, and so much more.

Granted, some people do have an even stronger negative bias than others. A 2014 study that appeared in the journal *Clinical Psychological Science* looked into the negativity we harbor when dealing with uncertainty, and it illustrated connections between uncertainty and rumination. We all want to resolve the uncertainties before us, but the person who is an intense ruminator is more acutely biased toward catastrophic thinking. In effect, he can become incapacitated by the worst-case scenario of what may come. The researchers also found that full-blown ruminators focus on themselves and their worries, creating a cycle of negative thinking. They immerse themselves in gloomy thoughts and are sure that Armageddon is coming.

Living with Not Knowing

People with a low tolerance for the unknown often feel the need for closure. They prefer what is predictable to keep a semblance of order. A 2018 study in the journal *Personality and Individual Differences* looked at people who measured highly in the need for closure and found that they are not great at divergent thinking.

Divergent thinkers are nimble at finding different ways to tackle a problem. They can come up with a multitude of ways to use a paperclip—for example, such an item can be used as a flathead screwdriver or to repair a broken zipper by sliding it through the tab and pulling. By contrast, the researchers found that subjects high in the need for closure felt less competent and experienced more negative emotions when solving divergent thinking tasks. If we want to think divergently and creatively, some tolerance over ambiguity and not knowing may be required. The ability to withstand uncertainty can make us more accepting and adaptable, giving us the freedom to learn and grow. To become more tolerant and divergent, we can start by being curious and asking questions. I often do this by jotting down questions in a notepad I carry around with me.

Other activities, such as storytelling and writing, can help us out of a hemmed-in and often negative mindset. Hearing a compelling narrative can help us embrace ambiguity. I appreciate a good yarn and can certainly embellish one. While we prepared the evening meal together, my mother often told a story about the old country. I would stop chopping the cabbage just to listen more carefully. Listening intently to a good tale got me outside of my head and into the shoes of the people in the story.

A study published in the *Creativity Research Journal* found that, after reading fiction, subjects are more tolerant of ambiguity, and having more tolerance keeps us from making snap judgments and regretful decisions. If we are okay with ambiguity, we may be able to reach outside ourselves and get out of our heads.

Write It Down

James Pennebaker is a professor emeritus of psychology at the University of Texas and the author of books about the benefits of writing, such as *Opening Up: The Healing Power of Expressing Emotions.* His research has found that regularly writing down our thoughts has positive health benefits, including improved immunity, reduced blood pressure and cholesterol, and fewer symptoms of depression and anxiety.

Many therapists suggest journaling to their patients for this very reason. A 2022 study published in the *Journal of the American Medical Association-Psychiatry (JAMA Psychiatry)*, found that written exposure therapy—under the care of a therapist—is effective in treating post-traumatic stress disorder. When a person repeatedly writes about a trauma that they experienced, they learn that the memory is not dangerous, and it can be recalled again and again with reduced distress over time. The repetitive exposure lessens the person's pain.

There are a few ways to establish a therapeutic writing routine:

- Set a time to write down what's on the top of your mind each day. This may feel awkward at first, but eventually, it will become a habit.
- There is no need to edit what you write.
- Don't try too hard or feel the need to be perfect.
- The act of writing itself is beneficial.
- There are different ways to journal. You can keep a diary, for example.
- Jot down dreams when you wake up.
- Use bullet points for organization.
- Doodling or illustrating your thoughts can help.
- Journaling for fifteen to twenty minutes a day can have the most benefits.

How to Combat "Musterbating"

Bemoaning what would have, should have, or could have been, not to mention what ought to be, is a type of inner noise many of us suffer from. This type of thinking was coined *musterbating* by the late psychologist Albert Ellis, who developed rational emotive behavior therapy and authored books like *The Road to Tolerance*. Like other forms of fatalistic thinking, musterbating emphasizes negativity in its wholly demanding nature. When we musterbate, we tell ourselves that we *must* do something. Examples of this kind of thinking are: "I *must* succeed." "I *must* be loved by this one person." "I *must* do better." "I *must* win." "I *must* have more."

Ellis contended that this very irrationality is the root of a lot of the emotional distress people experience. We cry over what we *must* make happen, leaving little room for constructive and solution-based thought. This is stubborn thinking at its core.

The person wallowing in such negative thoughts has an unreasonable belief system; it's the foundation of a rigid approach to life. Expectations are not met, and the distressed person struggles with the reality that she cannot control the actions of others or the situations and circumstances that come about. In the end, this person is left with feelings of failure.

For Ellis, no outcome would make everything in life *all better*. Winning the object of our affection's love or landing a coveted job may make everything better for a little while, but not for the long haul. In truth, adding such a premium on a desired result can backfire. Situations in life are not forever. What we think we must have today may not even be what we want tomorrow. Ellis noted that people construct their negative feelings, and luckily they can deconstruct them by deploying open and logical thinking and by replacing irrational thoughts with rational ones.

My Hui cousins, in our homeland of Northwest China, don't slosh around in what could have been or ought to be. Instead, they frequently use the expression *bai le*, (败了), a saying used to convey *defeat*. However, this saying means much more than defeat. It's used to express *Let it go. Oh, well. That's too bad.* He missed the train. *Bai le.* She didn't get the job. *Bai le.* The husband left his wife. *Bai le.* It applies to both minor and major events. In Western cultures, one would not be inclined to say, "Oh, too bad" about the dissolution of a marriage. Yet the concept of *bai le* is neither flippant nor callous; it accepts that hardship is part of our everyday existence. *Bai le* is in line with Ellis's idea that we must be tolerant about life and its ambiguities. He must have been a little Asian.

To become more tolerant of life's unpredictable surprises,

we can learn from other cultures. Many other cultures are better at ambiguity and not knowing. They know that life is interdependent and interconnected, and they handle uncertainty by watching how life unfolds. Accepting how life can be fickle is, perhaps, the most critical truth. Nothing is fixed and everything is moving. When we make plans, for example, we can be more open to changing them. Resisting change can make the uncertainty worse, perhaps even immobilize us from forward momentum. Our willingness to tolerate life as it comes can help us. The mind geared toward acceptance is fine with a little, or a lot of, ambiguity.

Another truth is that we are not the sum of our negative thoughts. A belief that life sucks may infect a person's underlying self-identity—*That guy is always a downer; he believes that every situation will result in the worst outcome ever.* When we are in this struggle, we may think that other people, like an intimate relationship, will ameliorate all our distress. However, no one can save us from the miseries inside our heads. We have to do it ourselves.

Albert Ellis's Advice

Demanding that something should have happened or must happen in a certain way is the essence of musterbating. Ellis's widely practiced Rational Emotive Behavior Therapy method is effective in dealing with anxiety, depression, intense anger, hypersensitivity, and other emotion regulation difficulties. He had some thoughts on how to combat our regrets and unreasonable internal demands:

- The world does not cooperate with our impossible requirements and expectations. However, refraining from absolutism will help us cope and problem-solve more effectively.

- It's good to dispute irrationality and put aside imperative thoughts like *must* and *should*. In Ellis's view, they are illogical, rigid, and unrealistic.
- Instead, we can reframe our thinking by viewing situations and events more positively.
- It's helpful to replace a rigid view of a situation with positive and accepting thoughts.
- We can do this, for example, by first visualizing a situation that gives us anxiety—"I will suck when I give my speech"—and then visualizing a positive outcome—"I am prepared to give my speech, and I am going to ace it."
- We can also replace our negative thoughts through humor. Levity can flip a switch and deescalate mental distress so that we can think about a situation positively.
- Accepting that what we get in life is what we get may also lead to less frustration and negativity.
- Acceptance does not mean it will be pleasant.
- Life situations can be well beyond our control. Knowing this may give us peace.

Managing uncertainty is hard when there are pandemics, wars, inflation, and continued political strife. It does not help that humans have a negative bias when faced with such difficulties. We tend to think the absolute worst will happen when life is filled with surprises.

This uncertainty can lead to rumination for some people

more prone to negativity, because we want order in our world, not unknowns piled onto more unknowns. Our irrationality about this is the cause of much emotional distress. Often, we cannot change circumstances. Life just is the way it is.

We are also irrational and intolerant of reality and the way things turn out. We want things to be different so that we can win and succeed without pain and discomfort.

However, because we construct our negative feelings, we can also deconstruct them. We can be positive, tolerant of ambiguity, and rid ourselves of the worries inside our heads.

Chapter Three

The Science of Emotions

Once, when I was wearing a long face, my dad remarked with an impish smile that I had a "face in mourning." His lesson: Don't take life so seriously. Likewise, my family never asked me, "Are you feeling happy today?" Such a question was antithetical to their way of thinking.

There is a general prejudice that negative emotions are bad and positive emotions are good. We spend a good deal of time negating half the emotions we experience because of this. One could argue that this narrow view of our emotional life might stunt our growth. Negative emotions are not the enemy. They are part of life just like the trees and the sky.

Uncertainty conjures up mixed feelings about what we think is supposed to happen or not. Illness, death, loss of livelihood, and other difficult events occur all the time, and these situations often leave us in an emotional quandary. The ups and downs of our moods can take us on a wild ride. Many of us torture ourselves with the extreme highs of happiness, only to sink into the excruciating lows of distress. It seems the lows would not be so low if the highs weren't so high.

Fortunately, when we can identify our emotional states, we can better regulate how we feel. This recognition can aid a person in remaining at an even mood level, neither in a state of uber elation, nor doom-and-gloom misery. My dad could give a practical description of a mood, and then he moved on. Ideally, one's life should be like a steady boat on calm waters, as well as on stormy seas. Some call this the Buddhist way, where we are tranquil like a monk through mindful thought and meditation. I try to make this my way, but I'm not always great at it.

Curiosity as a Path to Accessing Emotions

Integrative and holistic medicine physician Chris Gilbert, author of *The Listening Cure: Healing Secrets of an Unconventional Doctor*, recommends Gestalt therapy as a way to access our emotions. The idea is to be curious about what we feel and think right now. Gestalt means *whole*, concentrating on all the parts—mind, body, and emotions. What is my body feeling at this very moment? What emotions do I have right now? Be curious. There are no set guidelines. The sessions are designed to fit the person.

In therapy, the patient might sit across from an empty seat called "the Gestalt chair," and imagine another person in it, perhaps a boss, a spouse, or a family member. With curiosity, the patient might take the role of the other person or be himself. The *interaction* between the chairs brings emotions and feelings into the present. We may even have many chairs for a board meeting—the happy chair, the sad, the frustrated, or the jealous, among others. The chair can help us:

- Access the moment with observational curiosity: "I feel muscle tension from stress."
- Come to terms with what is happening within: "I feel frustrated with my job."
- Look at ourselves with interest: "When I see my neighbor, what is my awkwardness about?"
- Ask ourselves questions without judgment: "Am I angry because I fear something?"

The Hedonic Treadmill

When we return to a set level of mood, the "hedonic treadmill," which I mentioned earlier, is at play. This term was coined in the 1970s and has been refined over the years. It's called a "treadmill" because each of us has a level of happiness we return to, no matter how high our highs or low our lows. Every person comes into this world with a set point of happiness, and roughly 50 percent of one's happiness level is innate. The remaining 50 percent depends on how we live—from eating right and sleeping well to staying active, connected, and grounded.

Take, for example, the winner of the Mega Millions lottery who, after a time of utter euphoria, returns to his regular job and goes about life as usual. One such person was Canadian Robert

Goertzen, who won $22 million in 2016 and then went back to work as a heavy equipment instructor in Kelowna, British Columbia. In doing so, we can argue that he returned to his set level of existence.

Life Is Suffering

Like everyone, I have had my moments of great joy—marriage, the birth of babies, a child's college graduation, the last tuition payment, and a child's wedding. I knew I would come down from these temporary highs, yet I still feel melancholy when the high moods sink. Following the Buddhist way is hard to do.

I've also had cry-my-eyes-out moments—the deaths of loved ones, divorce, and serious illness. The suffering has been so great that, at times, I did not feel I would ever be right again. I felt an emotional pain that deadened my senses. Nothing tasted right, flowers smelled like cardboard, and the sun would never shine.

Fortunately, time does heal the pain. With every passing day, our numbed senses start to notice the little things—the smell of tea brewing or the sound of an infant crying. And finally, when time passes, the sun does poke through the dark clouds.

We all know that no one can run from life's painful moments. Therefore, why do I still feel shock and surprise whenever there's hardship? I realize I have to sit with what I feel and that pain and suffering can make the joyful moments feel ever more joyful. We need to feel *all* of life's emotions in order to live a rich life.

It helps to be a fluid and flexible thinker, one who accepts negative states as they are. Fluid thinkers are less rigid and tend to reason quickly, problem-solve effectively, and avoid roiling in catastrophe and disaster. Their thinking readily embraces emotions, from cheerful to dark, without too much angst and turmoil. My neighbor is a fluid and flexible thinker. She once went to a job interview for a position she very much wanted. She called me after her appointment and seemed both sad and hopeful. Even though she did not get the job, she decided it was a teachable moment that helped her to do better on her next interview.

Positive and Negative Emotions Need Each Other

A balance of emotions can make a difference in every domain of life, from love to work. Take sadness and happiness, for example. We can't feel real happiness unless we experience real sadness. How would a person know what extraordinary joy means if they fear and avoid sadness? Without experiencing both happiness and sadness the ability to experience either emotion is limited. Many emotions have a flip side—fear and courage, excitement and apathy, pride and humility. For instance, anger can motivate us to do great things, but spiraling out of control isn't at all useful. Being positive and hopeful when embarking on a start-up is good, but a little pessimism is useful as well, as it helps to set realistic expectations. And in our closest relationships, we might feel delight and love one minute and pain the next.

The push and pull of the relationships dear to us can be maddening. Carlin Flora, science writer and the author of *Friendfluence: The Surprising Ways Friends Make Us Who We Are*, has noted that we can suffer dissonance in our close relationships. We contend with paradoxes and mixed feelings about the people we love, for example. We cherish our close family and friends, yet they make us crazy with frustration. With this dissonance, "we might also feel guilt for negative feelings about our loved ones, which adds another layer of discomfort," she said. This dichotomy of emotions is ever-present in our relationships. We should be alert to the mind's tendency to hamstring us. It is not designed to deal with discordance.

Perhaps seeking one emotion over the other should not be the end goal. Working toward a sense of calm and peace may be a better aim. There are some ways to do this:

- Trying to better regulate our emotions, even though we cannot control what happens around us.
- Not hiding how we feel, especially from ourselves.
- Pinpointing what caused a particular emotion can bring a better understanding of ourselves.
- Opening up to all our emotional experiences can also bring a better understanding of ourselves.
- Being a little Buddhist. Our emotions are impermanent, and that this too shall pass.

What We Feel, Others Feel

In my formative years, I tried to leave my mother alone as much as possible when she was feeling down. A proper Hui girl was taught not to ask the adults too many questions or ask any questions at all. I never queried my mom because she told me to be quiet. I did, however, save many questions for my dad and sister, as they didn't seem to mind my curiosity.

Children learn to regulate their emotions from their parents, and they intuitively know that moods are contagious. A person's low and high moods can glom onto the people within reach. One person can infect an entire household. A "downer" disposition can be passed down through the generations. Many factors can contribute to depression, according to several sources, including the National Library of Medicine. However, if we have a first-degree relative who has depression like a parent or a sibling, we are two to three times at greater risk for the disorder. It may be even higher for major depressive disorder.

As a child, I would look in the mirror and wonder if I was feeling glum like my mother. Mom knew she tended to be somber—she had left her family and homeland for a strange land, one where she felt out of place—but she tried her best to set a good example for the rest of us, quietly going about the business of running a household, no matter what her mood level. This kind of effort counts for a lot.

Ron Friedman, formerly a professor at the University of Rochester and the author of *The Best Place to Work: The Art and Science of Creating an Extraordinary Workplace*, has studied the phenomenon of viral emotions. A reason for this contagion may be mimicry through the mirror neuron system that activates when we observe the moods of others around us. We unconsciously mimic others—for example, we yawn when the person sitting next to us yawns. In Friedman's research, he showed that if we sit in a room with a highly motivated person, our motivation is affected in a good way, and if we sit in a room with an unmotivated person, our motivation is affected in a bad way. This can happen just by being in the other person's presence, regardless of whether we talk to that person or not.

How to Regulate What We Feel

A neighbor of mine found herself in the unenviable position of attending her best friend's fiftieth birthday party, and she knew her ex-husband would be there, in tow was his new shiny second wife. My neighbor could have bowed out, but best friends are best friends, and she bolstered herself admirably. In the end, she deployed compassion, grace, resilience, and effective emotion regulation. She radiated this toward others and within herself as well. At one point, she even sat beside the new wife and chatted about innocuous things like recipes and gardening hacks. My friend later told me with her hand on her heart, "Being alive isn't easy, but I think everything is going to be okay. I'm glad I went."

Psychologists Todd Kashdan of George Mason University and Robert Biswas-Diener study the science of having a bright outlook in many corners of the world and from many different angles. (Biswas-Diener is known as the "Indiana Jones of positive psychology" for his research with groups such as the Amish, the Inuit, and the Maasai.) In their book, *The Upside of Your Dark Side*, they explore the gloom we run from, and how we shun sadness and disappointment as complete and total negatives. Most people want to be happy and sunny, not angry or depressed or whatever difficult emotion feels bad.

Yet, according to Kashdan and Biswas-Diener, heavy emotions shouldn't be cast aside. After all, focused anger can spur fairness and justice. Where would the civil rights movement be without righteous indignation? It fires us up. People who boldly speak their minds shine a light on themselves. We need only show the right amount of anger to get ahead. However, we have to be careful not to lose our heads.

Likewise, the prickly emotion of envy can urge us to do better. Coveting the neighbor's slim waistline may motivate us to hit the gym. And feeling mortified and regretful about a past action with a loved one can push us to make amends, to do better, and to be better. Certainly, good things can result from hard emotions.

Kashdan and Biswas-Diener have even argued, "Experiencing your full range of emotions affords you a fuller, richer life." It's better to be unafraid of shedding tears and embracing discomfort wholeheartedly than keeping emotions bottled up. Unhappiness is part of life, and we have to get used to it. Accepting sadness as much as joy forces us to see every emotion holistically, as all of them are intertwined.

Emotions inform us. If we are anxious, for instance, our brain is telling us that there may be danger. Jealousy tells us that we may be deficient and soon be abandoned. Shame tells us that we did something that needs correcting. Understanding all our states of being can create a richer existence. These are the instruments of self-awareness and therapy, and they can help us live a life that is slower, more empathic, peaceful, and harmonious. We can all learn from this open, optimistic thinking.

How to View Guilt and Shame

Humans are innately concerned with the threat of being ex-communicated from our social network. Evolution makes us abide by the rules of our group; otherwise, we might be thrown to the wolves. Feelings of guilt and shame come about after we think we have done something wrong, or when someone else tells us we have made a mistake. Guilt equals *I did something bad*, while shame equals *I am something bad*. Guilt is more straightforward to handle, but shame is harder, as we sometimes try to hide our shame.

According to much research, guilt and shame have prosocial characteristics. In one 2017 study from the journal *Frontiers in*

Psychology, researchers found that guilt can encourage a person to act morally in the future. In the instance of shame, some people can become avoidant, but on the whole, they become motivated to do better.

When we feel one of these emotions, we often try to make amends, give apologies, and generally do better for others. Yet shame is more problematic because of its identity-defining feelings of worthlessness and self-loathing. Cross-examination from a boss, for example, can be an entirely uncomfortable experience because the boss is in a position of power and can make the employee feel ashamed. This dynamic can result in a less fruitful and less positive work experience. Shame is an emotion often mixed with self-criticism, depression, anxiety, and other negative feelings—even anger. When a person carries shame, they can have a barren self-view. This self-evaluation can be harsh, leading to low self-worth. Negativity about the self can pervade work, intimacy, and friendships. We may be required to balance this negative self-view with a more realistic take.

How a person was raised has much to do with guilt and shame. Guilt and shame are felt more when one's needs for safety and belonging have not been met. Religiosity and culture, for example, can have an outsized effect on how we experience certain emotions. When I was younger, I did what I was told, following directives that were rooted in religion and culture. It was the only way for me to feel safe. Of course, I was also inwardly conflicted. *Why is eating with the right hand important?* I thought. *What about left-handed people?* Growing up with rules about religion can be wholly confusing and even somewhat disturbing.

A person can carry this confusion and distress around

well into adulthood, making the idea of letting go and finding peace within unattainable. In adulthood, as I was wising up to illogical decrees from my childhood, I thankfully rode the guilt-and-shame carousel less and less.

Countering emotions like shame, guilt, and regret can be hard, but it's not impossible. We must be aware that we are feeling them, and knowing that we are innately biased toward negative thinking can help.

Emotions like shame and guilt percolate in the subconscious, giving a person the feeling of underlying dread and inadequacy. However, if we identify the emotion, we can better handle the emotion. Matthew Lieberman, a psychology professor at UCLA and the director of the Social Cognitive Neuroscience Lab, noted that labeling how we feel can help lessen the intensity of how we feel. Handling our emotions this way can quiet the part of the brain linked to emotional response.

We are also healthier if we can express our emotions positively. This awareness can help us deploy much-needed self-compassion. If we want a healthier self-view, validation must start with us. We need to accept ourselves as we are and start looking at our emotions differently. We have to:

- Pinpoint the emotion we are feeling.
- Name the emotion and how we feel—angry and fearful, tense and upset—say it out loud or write it down.
- Don't react to it. Sit with it and get to know it, even if it is uncomfortable. Sometimes, focusing on bodily sensations can help us be present with the discomfort of the emotion.
- We can be alert to our urge to deny and push away

the emotion, whether it's eating too many slices of chocolate cake or downing a bottle of whiskey.
- Practice self-compassion by putting a hand on our chests and breathing deeply.

We Have to Work Through Our Feelings Ourselves

The best way to manage our feelings is to face them head-on and work through them. This, of course, does not mean that we should take them out on other people.

A person who is not grounded may not have a good handle on regulating their moods and may have a hard time lessening the severity of what they feel. To counter this, they can try "down-regulation," something that therapists use in the therapeutic setting. For example, feeling angry about getting rear-ended doesn't mean we should have an intense shouting match with the offender. Down-regulating can be like shifting the gears of a manual car, where we consciously shift the emotion down a notch.

Meanwhile, the opposite of this is "up-regulation," or revving up emotions when needed. Our softball coach wants us to be supercharged about the upcoming game, so getting pepped up may help us score a home run.

Emotion research pioneer James Gross, a professor and director of the Stanford Psychophysiology Lab, studied the idea that emotions can be modulated. We can deploy tools to adjust our emotions at different intervals. When we sense the emotion before it comes on, we can alter and regulate it. During the moment of feeling an emotion, we can assign how we will respond.

How to Manage the Ups and Downs

Like my friend and her ex at the birthday party, being aware of how we feel and adjusting ourselves to the situation at hand, like James Gross suggests, can help. This calibration can affect both the mind and the body. Here are five ways to do this:

- *Choose the situation:* "I will not dine at that particular restaurant because I want to avoid my ex, who is a frequent patron."
- *Modify the situation:* "I have to attend my nephew's wedding, but I can sit away from my ex."
- *Be aware of physical responses:* "Is my heart racing? If it is, I will take a deep breath."
- *Interpret the situation with logic:* "I may be nervous, but no one is watching. People are too concerned about themselves—not me."
- *Embrace the emotional response:* Get acquainted with discomfort rather than suppressing it: "I can drown myself in alcohol, but I'm not going to do that. I will sit with the discomfort I feel."

We cannot control what happens in life, but we can try to manage our emotions and reactions. This is better for us and everyone around us. We can make better use of how we feel. Instead of lashing out in anger when we have been wronged, we can figure out what the anger is telling us. For me, my reactions to unpleasant situations may be a fear of abandonment. We are inclined to think that negative emotions, like sadness and disappointment, are the enemy.

However, all our moods and emotions, both negative and positive, are an important part of life. Instead of fighting our emotions, like anxiety or anger, we can be curious about what we feel. Being curious can inform us and help us become less rigid and more fluid thinkers. This will help us reason and problem-solve more quickly and effectively. Less rigidity lets us face how we feel, and as a result, it can help us regulate how we feel. Feeling and embracing all of life's emotions with tranquility and mindful thought can lead to a more meaningful life.

Chapter Four

The Truth About Failure and Self-Sabotage

I know a young man who strived, sweated, and persevered to join Major League Soccer teams. He played soccer with the best. He was fast, talented, hard-working, and competed in the company of champions. Yet, through no fault of his own, he ultimately didn't make the cut, even though he had done the best he could. After that, he pivoted from soccer and went on to earn a doctorate in public health. I would say this was an excellent adaptation.

This reminded me of the Hui word *suanli* (酸了), which means "sour" and is used when someone needs to give up and move on. The idea of *suanli* is similar to the Japanese concept of *shoganai*, which means "the matter cannot be helped." Another term the Hui use is *mei banfa* (没办法), meaning there is "no method." Giving up is regarded as acceptable if there is *no method* or way forward. These terms are used to acknowledge the disappointment of a situation, and if there is nothing to be done to ameliorate it, everyone moves on. There isn't a cheering squad telling us to push through our defeats to get to the other side. There is no point in pursuing something that has gone *sour*. Accepting failure and moving on is *mei banfa*.

The feeling of failure often accompanies emotions like shame and guilt. In modern society, we are set up to feel like we do not measure up. Just scrolling through someone else's social media feeds can make us feel depressed. Nowadays people promote themselves like they're saleable brands. This has gotten so bad that some health professionals would like to see a form of "selfie-itis" listed in the *Diagnostic and Statistical Manual of Mental Disorders*.

Does constant self-promotion do a number on a person's self-image and expectations? David Brooks, the *New York Times* columnist and the author of several books including *The Road to Character*, has written about individualism and self-esteem and how it can distort our expectations and how we see ourselves. Our culture emphasizes how I have to be loudly *me*. Pride appears to have taken over, leading to feelings of entitlement and superiority. Perhaps, this is a way to offset failure.

Of course, children bear the brunt of this. They are pushed into thinking that they can be anything or anyone they want to be—that is the American dream, after all. TikTok influencer fame is within reach. Some young people are being taught that they are the best, are piled with loads of self-esteem, and are protected from hardships and difficulties. Certainly, some personal confidence is needed, but confidence in excess can be harmful. A person who thinks he's superior to others will most definitely suffer when he is dealt the blow of reality that he is ordinary, just like the rest of us. Certainly, one could argue that some people—like Wolfgang Amadeus Mozart, Leonardo da Vinci, and Ray Kurzweil—were or are extraordinary and exceedingly accomplished. However, this doesn't make them better than the next person.

Many researchers, including Mark Leary, a professor at Duke University and the author of *The Curse of the Self: Self-Awareness, Egotism, and the Quality of Human Life*, have studied how people generally tend to *think* they are more attractive, smarter, and better than others. In effect, we are predisposed to our very own awesomeness. Leary's research found that people think they are right two-thirds of the time. That's why people may readily dismiss opposing viewpoints by thinking, *I am always right. Why do I need to listen to anyone else?*

Seeing Failure for What It Is, and Not Much More

Evolutionary psychologist Glenn Geher surmises that we have to think about failure as something other than a personal flaw. "The most successful among us are the people who have failed the most," he says. A person who has been through hardship, he argues, will be less inclined to buckle when an obstacle stands in the way of his progress.

People who have lived through disappointments—that is, those who haven't been completely beaten down and broken by life—might know something about the truths of life and may be more willing to learn and grow. They may be more likely to accept their setbacks and move on. When a person is handed a hardship, the brain must rewire itself and learn something new.

People who are more prone to negativity may ruminate about their failures, while others try not to think about them. But we do have to parse, rather than dwell on, each failure and the information it provides for success the next time around. Some people romanticize failure and turn it into a platitude or a badge of honor, as in "We must fail in order to succeed." According to the work of Roman Krznaric, author of *Carpe Diem Regained*, we've blunted failure when we do this, as if failure is the path to the promised land. Is there always a silver lining when failure strikes? No. Sometimes we just fail. Glamorizing and indulging in our failure does not move us forward. My mother used to quip, "When you done complain, go sweep floor." I think she was right about seeing failure as a fact of life and little more. It just happens, and there's nothing romantic about falling flat on our faces.

Accepting bad news is good, as acceptance is central to healthy positive thought, all of which leads to psychological growth and necessary brain rewiring.

Becoming unglued or romanticizing a defeat is the antithesis of a thoughtful approach to failure. Self-reflection is useful in terms of addressing a mistake, but it can also lead to ruminating in negativity, and ruminating inside our heads is a precursor to depressive thinking. It's best to take a compassionate no-nonsense view. In effect, let's give ourselves a break and take an open view of defeat. Consider the following:

- Failure is not bad. It's useful, inevitable, and good.
- If you are fussing over your performance, think about your purpose instead.
- If difficult emotions are present, tap into your physical

sensations. Notice the thoughts that may come up, and then let them go.

- Instead of overthinking and ruminating, take what you learned, use new strategies, and move on.
- If you fail, fail again, many times.
- Gather your failures like they're working capital.

Hard-and-fast thinkers want perfection, and defeat and failure are not in their vocabulary. They have the idea that everything must be *just so.* However, *no one* is perfect. Thinking that we can be perfect is the path to definite failure.

My parents were exacting about certain things in life, but not all. For example, my father handled his brush, ink, and rice paper meticulously during his calligraphy sessions. My mother was exacting in the kitchen. The rice had to be washed three times and the vegetables scrubbed just as much. This type of perfection, fortunately, did not rule other areas of their lives. My parents were surprisingly hands-off about many things. Namely, they never once pestered me about bringing home straight-As, not that grades weren't important. Frankly, I was studious just *enough.* Perhaps my parents knew that demanding a straight-A report card was plain old crazy-making for them and me.

The Rise of Perfectionism

Parents who expect a certain level of perfection use their children as vehicles for their own fulfillment. These parents end up raising offspring who become too focused on themselves, thinking failure will ruin their lives. While they're careful about not making mistakes, they're missing out on valuable lessons. Such self-focus isn't a great backdrop for development. The perfectionist is closed-minded in thinking and behavior, and she is ever concerned that she may lose the validation of her parents, as well as their affection and love.

According to Peter Gray, a psychologist and research professor at Boston College, as well as the author of *Free to Learn*, there is little freedom in modern-day education, and no autonomy to learn or to be curious. While children are innately curious, we do a good job of stamping it out, he has argued. Genuine curiosity is a trait that's accepting of life. In effect, we open our eyes to find wonder and novelty in the world; it is the opposite of indifference and hard-and-fast beliefs. (I should thank my parents for their hands-off approach.)

Curiosity is a big part of positive psychology. When we *want* to learn new things, we are engaged with life, which fuels fulfillment and well-being. When we are curious, the worry of failure and perfection fall away. Curious people tend to be happier and less neurotic, while the unengaged and disinterested tend to be negative and depressed.

Children innately have plenty of wonder in them, and this drives their motivation and desire to figure out how the world works. We can relearn this intuitive trait by opening our eyes, paying attention to what we see, and wondering out loud. Asking an open-ended question about what we are looking at is a good start. For some people, this may take being uncomfortable; it's a willingness to be wrong and say, "I don't know." Doing so can feel unpleasant, but it does not have to take us on a spin down the negativity spiral.

Nowadays, we prepare children for standardized testing through rote memory, competition, and subject-focused learning. It's an environment that can deaden children. They do not learn to be curious and open. Gray wants to see children utilize their critical thinking, deep understanding, collaborative nature, and a sense of inquisitive engagement.

A meta-analysis (a review of multiple studies on a topic) from the University of Bath and York St. John University in the United Kingdom, found a rise in perfectionism in more recent years. The cause of this increase may have resulted from various factors, including social comparison through social media and the rise of individualism and decrease in collectivism. Not only has the demand for perfection by others steadily increased, but the demands we make on ourselves have increased as well. The results of a meta-analysis are normally strong and reliable because it is a consolidation of data from previous peer-reviewed studies; its primacy is the data analysis of many multiple subjects.

According to research that was published in 2006 in the *Journal of Cognitive Psychotherapy*, people who look for things to go wrong in life leave a door open to depressiveness, a hallmark of perfectionist thinking. Psychologists view such a thought process as a cause of anxiety and other mood disorders. It is a frame of mind that also stokes other mental illnesses, including substance abuse, depression, and eating disorders. The link between perfectionism and eating disorders is real, according to the journal *Clinical Psychology Review*. While there is a chicken-and-egg problem in deciphering this—who knows whether perfectionism feeds the eating disorder or vice versa—the link is clear. Among tween and teenage girls, perfectionism can be tied to the desire for a thin waistline and an "amazing" boyfriend.

Perfectionism Leads to Close-Minded Thinking

Perfectionism is a cautionary perspective that keeps a person from taking risks. However, a certain amount of risk-taking is necessary in life. Trying new things is good for growth and well-being. A closed mindset can drown out curiosity and creativity, the antithesis of what the modern world demands.

The drive to be perfect may even lead someone to feel like a fake. Although "imposter syndrome" is not actually a syndrome, nor is it listed in the *Diagnostic and Statistical Manual of Mental Disorders*, it is a fairly common phenomenon. Even the famous and ultra-successful can have an underlying feeling of grave inadequacy. They may think that their achievements are not real and their accolades are unearned, or that dumb luck was on their side. This tendency is, sometimes, related to neuroticism—a problematic personality trait associated with negative states like anxiety, self-consciousness, and emotional instability—where we watch over our shoulders waiting to be unmasked.

Perfectionism is not the same as a healthy striving to do our best. Instead, the desire for flawlessness can lead to self-sabotage. When we aim for a perfect result, we may focus on every little detail. For example, being thorough is good but not if it makes us hand in a work project two weeks after the deadline. The goal of never making a mistake is tied to the fear of failure. Perfectionists have trouble living up to their own expectations.

Stop the Self-Sabotage

When I was small, my American-ness rubbed up against my Hui-ness. I remember remarking to my dad that life was *always* going to be unfair for me and loads of other people *never* had it as hard as I did. My dad was quick to point out my faulty thinking and my use of words like *always*, *never*, and *forever*. "Why do you use these words?" he asked. "Some days are hard, and some days are not, for all people." Then he sat at the kitchen table, sipping his tea as if he were a monk sitting cross-legged on a mountaintop. To him, life was about acceptance and not being boxed in. I didn't hear him utter my *forever* kind of language. Instead, he peppered his conversations with possibilities and set aside anything that seemed remotely permanent.

Over time, I have found that it is best to get out of my own way. Being my own worst enemy can lead to self-sabotaging behaviors and negative states of mind. Self-doubt, for example, can morph into procrastination, or worse, paralysis.

We may feel that, even though we do not suffer from a clinically diagnosed mental illness like crippling depression, severe anxiety, or any debilitating emotional disorder, we still do not have the life we want to live. Or we may have religiously attended therapy for *years*, yet find ourselves hiding from our emotions and what we truly feel. Meanwhile, we sense we've been sabotaging ourselves with negative self-talk. Week in and week out, we find ourselves sitting across from the therapist with a new catastrophe that needs immediate attention—the boss dismissed the project, the friend didn't call back, or the partner is brooding over a remark. We might ask ourselves, "When will I be living the emotionally satisfying existence that I deserve?"

Self-sabotaging thought processes can come in many forms, including absolutist thinking. The person who suffers from this kind of cognitive distortion uses words like *forever*, *all*, and *worst*. Essentially, words like these can halt open thinking.

This mental trap is deployed by depressed and anxious people regularly. Research published in the journal *Clinical Psychological Science* looked at this type of thought distortion and analyzed dozens of Internet forums. They examined absolutism in the use of language. The investigators found that forums for depression, anxiety, and suicidal ideation showed the highest number of absolutist words—including *always*, *totally*, *entire*, *never*, or *nothing*. Not surprisingly, suicidal ideation contained the most usage.

For sufferers of cognitive distortion, this type of thinking can invade all areas of life. In relationships: "You always think about yourself and never about me." In the workplace: "My project was a complete failure." And in health: "I blew my diet with that donut, so I might as well eat all of them." These sufferers tend to be unrealistic about life in general, hard on themselves and others, often demanding what is unattainable.

We Don't Have to Thwart Ourselves

There are many ways to foil ourselves if we are self-saboteurs. We might put things off, overeat, self-medicate, or avoid hard emotions. These can be nuanced and subtle behaviors we might not even notice, but they are there.

Self-sabotage often comes with a dose of cognitive dissonance. In many areas of life, we contend with this type of mental discord. Cognitive dissonance is mental disharmony that happens when one's behavior flies in the face of proven fact, like the party guy who knows that drinking a bottle of bourbon in one evening is bad for his health but does it anyway because he thinks it is part of his identity. Some standard examples of the disconnect between behavior and belief include:

- Smoking, even though you know it causes cancer.
- Driving a large, gas-powered SUV, even though you want to be energy efficient.
- Eating cake and ice cream every night, even though you want to lose weight.
- Knowing you have a project due but are sitting on the couch procrastinating.

Experts have studied procrastination as a form of self-sabotage—in fact, perfectionism and procrastination go hand in hand. Tim Pychyl, a retired professor of psychology at Carleton University in Canada and the author of *Solving the Procrastination Puzzle: A Concise Guide to Strategies for Change*, studies the art of putting things off and notes that this habit resides somewhere between one's intent and one's action, and bringing the two together is thorny for those who tend to stall. According to Pychyl, we are less responsible toward the self than we are toward others; most of us show up for a friend, more or less arriving at the agreed-upon time, yet a similar sense of responsibility is lost on the self. For instance, we intend to exercise at a designated hour but instead roll over in bed and hit the snooze button.

As with other self-sabotaging behaviors, delay is often a problem of emotion regulation. Tasks that we put off and avoid come with emotional states, such as anxiety, frustration, and resentment. We often run from our negative emotions. We just don't know how to handle them, let alone know what to do with them. It's so much easier to close our eyes and wish the tasks away, but it's wiser to face them and the feelings that go along with them.

Our brains are pre-programmed to put off certain tasks automatically. Research published in the *Journal of Consumer Research* found that we attend to urgent tasks that take less time (as in, "the plant will die if I don't water it right now") and put aside important tasks that are more involved (as in, "if I don't finish that project, I won't get promoted"). Important tasks are often harder and take longer, whereas urgent tasks are often easier and give a feeling of reward when completed. Therefore, we prefer to work on the urgent tasks first, and then turn to important tasks much later. Yet sometimes, later keeps getting pushed further into the future. According to psychologist Seth Gillihan from the University of Pennsylvania and the author of *Mindful Cognitive Behavioral Therapy*, "this tactic translates to *Delay Transforms into Relief*."

It's a reinforcement of the habit I call *I Want to Avoid that Unenjoyable Task*. It's self-defeating behavior to be sure, and it's the kind that guarantees failure. Sometimes, it's easier to fail than to succeed because we want people to know that the task lacked our *effort*, not our *ability*.

There are simple actions we can take to combat a tendency to handicap ourselves:

- Make a plan. Being uncertain or unsettled can increase self-sabotaging behaviors, but making a plan and setting realistic goals can counter this. *I will forgo cake after dinner.*
- Start small. We tend to go big: *I am signing up for the marathon.* However, we should start small: *Today, I will do five push-ups. Tomorrow, I will do ten.*
- Know what we value. *I want to live a healthy life.*

Our values guide the direction we are heading. Values shape personal identity.

- Replace the habit. Instead of snacking on junk food, stock the fridge with healthy choices, like fruits and nuts.

My father did not delay or torment himself with self-sabotaging behaviors. Avoiding an unenjoyable task would have been a luxury for him. My parents fled their homeland as refugees and lived with hardship for a decade, and my mainland Hui kin lived through periods of national strife, cultural reform, and rehabilitation camps, which were really prisons similar to the reported camps we hear about in Northwest China where many Uyghurs are held today. The hardships my people have had to endure put life into sharp perspective for me. When lives are at stake, why would I want to wallow in my miseries?

Certainly people who have lived through hardship can suffer post-traumatic stress disorder or be bitter and resentful. However, after hardship, some may have a different view of what matters in life. In my father's case, the idea that other people might sabotage themselves through self-medicating, engaging in unhealthy eating, indulging in poor sleep hygiene, or any number of self-inflicted behaviors probably seemed thoughtless to him. Yet, these types of problems are very real and common.

We Stuff Ourselves Silly

I once walked by a sign that read THE BUFFET OF BUFFETS, 5 BUFFETS IN 24 HOURS, and thought, *Who would want to eat that much?* Yet gorging ourselves with food seems to be an American pastime. According to the Pew Research Center, the average

American eats 23 percent more than he did in the 1970s. Certainly, some people are emotional eaters, and this helps them cope with stress or negative moods. If we feel bad about ourselves, we might eat to feel better, and this can become a habit.

Diet and nutrition researchers are now on a mission to cut our portions because we are terrible at portion control. If we visit a roadside service area, the largest beverage container holds thirty-two ounces. In contrast, a large cup in Europe contains about 8.4 ounces, and a small cup is around half that size. Of course, Europeans are thinner, and this may be one of the reasons why.

Our biology comes with a built-in problem, however: The human body has been instructed by evolution to store food. Just as we are predisposed to negativity, we are wired to eat. For ancient humans, lean times were always just ahead, food was not always plentiful, and humans had to efficiently gather food and fight off predators. Our caveman ancestors didn't need to count calories, nor did they have to battle with processed foods, preservatives, and heavy carbs. While exercising caution about what and how much we eat is a modern-day necessity, this action is in direct opposition to our prehistoric instincts—something called "evolutionary mismatch." We are supposed to eat *a lot* and store that fat.

It's also a cruel trick that our bodies crave the sugary, fatty, and salty—exactly what processed foods contain—not to mention ingredients we cannot pronounce like sodium nitrite and sodium benzoate. Is it even a surprise that more processed food is consumed in the US than in any other nation? Frozen dinners, microwave pizzas, and packaged cookies are convenient and filled with things that are bad for us and yet very hard to pass up. Processed food may taste good, but we have higher rates of obesity, heart disease, high blood pressure, and diabetes because of it.

In addition, the body is pre-programmed not to squander energy and keep its fat reserves. Certainly, the couch looks good compared to the gym. Why get up and move? The body does not want to waste energy.

A person is better off defying their evolutionary instincts and stepping back to ask: "Will eating this giant fudge sundae help me reach my goal weight?" "Will drinking this fifth can of beer be consistent with living a long life?" If we value well-being, then no, that sundae and that beer are at odds with our goals. The way we interact with our emotions and behaviors matters.

Countless research has been done on healthy behaviors. The Harvard Medical School's landmark Grant Study of Adult Development has followed hundreds of men over many decades. (Women were not part of the study when it began in 1938, as Harvard was still an all-male school.) This ongoing study now covers new generations of the original participants, with their wives and children included. It has examined important aspects of well-being. Plus, some of its early subjects went on to careers in the public sector—including President John F. Kennedy and *Washington Post* editor Ben Bradlee. Here are some findings about negative, unhealthy habits from the study:

- People who experience relationship satisfaction at age fifty are physically healthy in their elder years.
- Loneliness increases sensitivity to physical pain.
- Loneliness suppresses our immunity and disrupts cognitive function.

- Emotional intelligence skills like empathy, altruism, and humor help people handle setbacks.
- Cigarette smoking and alcoholism are the greatest contributors to early morbidity and death.

Be Aware of the Unhealthy Path

Negative habits can become so entrenched in day-to-day life that doing something to counteract these behaviors feels like a constant battle.

Paying attention to what sets off our bad habits is important in stopping them. Do you tend to smoke after a meal? Do you overeat when you visit your parents? This awareness can reveal the causes. When we identify what the cause is, we can move toward managing and overcoming our self-sabotaging behaviors. To do this, we have to distinguish our thoughts from our emotions. This will help us pinpoint patterns in behavior. We might discover that a stressful day at work often leads to one too many cupcakes.

Once we are aware of what we are doing, we are better able to cope and develop strategies that work for us. For example, if cupcakes are a downfall, we can walk out of our way to avoid the bakery. Removing the temptation sets us up for an automatically healthy response. It's a rejiggering that can help build up our self-control. There are ways to be more aware:

- When and where does your unwanted behavior occur?
- Who are you with when this behavior occurs?
- What is the payoff of your behavior?
- Monitor this behavior and understand why you are doing it.

- Form a mental image of a future event that may set off this behavior.
- Imagine how you would prefer to behave.

How Does Negative Thinking Affect Us?

I knew a woman who was unable to conquer her self-destructive habits. She operated with negative filters *all the time*. For her, everything was bad, people were wrong, life was a pain, and her partner was never going to change. These are the same things I heard her say again and again. This negative thinking held her back, and to numb her pain, she gorged herself on food. I tried to get her to engage in activities instead of eating, like taking a walk to the nearby park or volunteering with me to pick up trash with the neighborhood charity, but she declined my entreaties. She died not long after in her seventies of heart disease.

She may have been an extreme case, but even the most optimistic among us aren't immune from general pessimism—it's just how the brain works. Somehow it seems easier to contemplate the good fortune that has passed us by. Many times I have thought, *My good luck might run out soon.*

A lot of people think pessimistically. "The rain will probably ruin our vacation." "Life would have been better if I got that job." This kind of mental tussle is also known as "discounting the positive," or "counterfactual thinking," which is highlighted in cognitive behavioral therapy. When we are in a negative frame of mind, we do not allow pleasant thoughts about occasions to seep in, even ones that normally invite excitement and joy. There are no rose-colored glasses, only ones tinted in gloomy gray.

Research published in the journal *Behaviour Research and Therapy* looked at this form of thinking and how people reflect on the past and anticipate the future through a somber lens. Thinking in this way means it is hard to seek the rewards of the things that are uplifting in life. Negative appraisals can become second nature. Even attending a joyful event like a wedding or a graduation can be reflected on with misery, *If only I hadn't opened my mouth that day, I am the biggest fool.* A different and more positive mental appraisal may be in order, *I may have gotten wet, but the morning air outside is wonderful.* When the mind is not boxed into an unenthusiastic framework of thinking, a person can learn and grow.

Self-Sabotage in the Extreme

About four in ten Americans experience anxiety or depression, according to a Kaiser Family Foundation report. However, island nations like the Solomon Islands and Papua New Guinea have among the lowest rates of depression at 3 percent or lower, according to the stats organization Data Pandas.

We do know that, for some people, happiness is fragile. Research published in the journal *Personality and Individual Differences* looked into this fragility—a sort of fear of happiness state of mind—whereby a person thinks that clutching happiness is a bad objective because awful things are always coming at us. Being miserable is what the person knows.

For these people, happy times may seem like a trap. They may be skeptical of bliss, suffer from the inability to enjoy pleasure (which is called "anhedonia"), and are more comfortable with tragedy, trauma, and misery. In the end, they seem unable to reach the solid ground of contentment. If every person has the potential to break your heart, they might argue, why bother reaching out to others for real connection?

These types of people may be able to access their feelings, but they may not *allow* themselves to feel good. They may think, *I do not deserve to feel happy.* They may think they have no right to experience compassion in any form, especially self-compassion. They may then waive happiness for hardened strength to give the impression that they can bear and withstand any difficulty—they are not frail. For some people, this tendency may be entrenched because they were dismissed or neglected by caretakers during their younger years.

In extreme cases, anhedonia can be a symptom of depression and other disorders like bipolar and post-traumatic stress. French psychologist Théodule Ribot described *l'anhédonie* or the disappearance of pleasure in 1896 as the opposite of *l'analgésie*, the absence of pain.

In other related cases, some people may suffer from alexithymia. While not a disorder, this suite of features highlights a person's inability to recognize emotions and feel their emotions, with empathy particularly hard to come by. A person with alexithymia may even be misdiagnosed with autism. If they feel discomfort and psychic pain, they may engage in behaviors to make that discomfort disappear. These behaviors may include impulsivity, emotional eating, binge drinking, or other self-destructive actions like self-mutilation.

Coined in the 1970s by psychiatrist Peter Sifneos, alexithymia is derived from Greek and means *having no words for emotions*. Approximately 12 percent of people have this trait, and individuals with alexithymia are more vulnerable to mental disorders, especially depressive ones. When a person with alexithymia is under mental or physical duress or both, they are more likely to say, "I am fine." They think they are fine because accessing emotions is not possible for them. The feeling of joy is, likewise, demobilized. If they do not know how to feel, they do not know how to feel good.

While most people do not suffer extreme cases of anhedonia or alexithymia, some people have felt a fear of happiness, as well as a degree of emotional numbness. When we experience, for example, the end of a painful relationship, we prefer not to ever live through that hurt again. Arming ourselves with emotional numbness sounds fine. However, this only works for the time being. Ideally, after grieving the end of a relationship, we can learn from it and move on to a better one the next time around.

Viewing Moods with Detachment

I would argue that, while complete emotional immobilization is harmful, some detachment might be good. The Buddha would approve of such detachment. Learning how to consider our emotions with an impartial eye may help. There is evidence that one can feel more neutral and less charged about emotional events. In one study, Japanese participants reported struggling with emotions less often than Americans do; they may be more detached from their emotions. In another study from the journal *Emotion*, Japanese subjects, when compared with American subjects, were found to feel more mixed emotions about pleasant situations; having such mixed emotions could be another form of detachment.

People perceive moods differently in other cultures. In other cultures around the world, feeling uncomfortable is just a part of normal living. When we confront a problem, we may want to blame ourselves, but removing the self from the equation could be helpful. We may be inclined to ask, "What is the matter with me?" We can ask instead, "What is wrong with the scenario I am in?" or, "How do I handle this difficult situation?"

Our negative mood states do not have to hamper or immobilize us. Certainly, modern-day living can handicap us and make us feel like we are failures. However, we don't have to beat ourselves up about it. Besides, the march toward perfection distorts our expectations and how we see ourselves. The alternative is preferable. If we think about failure differently, we can learn from our mistakes and disappointments. Instead of caving in the face of a setback, we can let the brain rewire itself, and our difficult experiences can inform us. We also know that our negativity and fear of failure can lead us to unwanted behaviors like self-sabotage. But procrastination, overeating, substance abuse, or any number of bad habits can be overcome if we pay attention to what we are doing and how we are reacting. Accepting our failures can help us out of misery.

Chapter Five

Having a Resilient Growth Mindset

My mother used to tell the story of how, at the turn of the twentieth century, Han soldiers captured my great-grandfather and decapitated him in the middle of the street in China. My great-grandmother was seized and spent many years as the concubine of the village gunpowder maker. She wasn't allowed an education or any means to earn a living. This was how the world worked then.

At the same time, the gunpowder maker did some things that were decent and right. For one, he owned a cow and asked my great-grandmother to milk it. She washed her hands, said a prayer, and sat on a wooden stool to soothe and coax the animal to produce. The neighbors came by to fill their pails with milk and dropped their coins into the till. After the first morning of milking, she handed the coins to the gunpowder maker.

He said, "The coins are yours."

The next day, she milked the cow, accepted the neighbors'

coins, and handed them to the gunpowder maker. He said the same thing, "The coins are yours." He said this day after day until she stopped handing over the money.

Pocketing this money gave her faith and permission to dream. In the end, my great-grandmother bought her freedom with the coins. The cow was her saving grace; it gave her hope and bolstered her resilience.

We had heard this story many times, and my sister added this notation in passing: "Hope is a good thing, but the right kind of hope is best. Just don't let that hope bleed into foolishness. That's another thing." My sister was twelve years older than I was, and much wiser than most people.

Resilience is the highly useful ability to bounce back from hard times. It helps us face fears, reframe a glum view, regulate emotions, problem-solve, be flexible, and focus on what can be done, among other positive behaviors. In addition, resilience protects us from what can beat us down. Resilient people can remain adaptable in the face of calamity and can, sometimes, even seem stronger than before a disaster.

The late Emmy Werner was among the earlier researchers who studied this topic. She was a professor emerita at the University of California, Davis, and the author of many books, including *Vulnerable, but Invincible: A Longitudinal Study of Resilient Children and Youth.* She studied children on the Hawaiian island of Kauai in the 1950s and found that among the many children who were raised in adverse conditions, including insecure households and being in the care of mentally ill parents, about a third became competent and caring adults. What helped these individuals were strong bonds and connections with a kind and compassionate adult—a teacher, a relative, or a caretaker.

Growth After Disaster

Along with Werner and other researchers, psychologists Richard Tedeschi and Lawrence Calhoun, both professors at the University of North Carolina, have continued the study of psychological growth after a shocking disaster or failure, and they found that positive personal development can come about after horrific adversity. Essentially, the proof is in the survivor—as in my great-grandmother's case. For example, someone who bravely fights cancer might feel she has been given extra time on Earth, and that sense of added time might help her gladly smell the roses every single day. This phenomenon is called "post-traumatic growth," in which the other side of trauma can lead survivors to change their perspectives, enhancing wisdom, gratitude, compassion, and generally focusing on what matters most in life.

Some researchers, such as psychologist Anthony Mancini, who heads the Trauma, Social Processes, and Resilience Lab at Pace University, wondered if such study results about post-traumatic growth have been accurate. Asking someone who has pulled through a catastrophe whether he is now a better person may be a flawed question. Often, studies use self-reported scales such as the Post-Traumatic Growth Inventory, which looks for positive responses in appreciation of life, relationships with others, new possibilities in life, personal strength, and spiritual change. However, self-reports may not be precise, Mancini has argued that a trauma survivor will certainly respond, "Yes, I am a better person now."

But is the survivor really a better person as a result of surviving trauma? Perceived growth and actual growth may be two different things. A 2009 study in the journal *Psychological Science* reported that perceived growth and actual growth appear unrelated. Researchers learned that perceived growth is associated with increased distress from a trauma experienced, but actual growth is related to decreased distress. This may mean that perceived and actual growth each reflect different processes. Largely, a person may perceive that they are better and have improved after a trauma, but knowing that they actually *are better* is difficult. How would we know what the person was like before their traumatic event? Researchers like Mancini feel that self-reports may not always portray behavior accurately.

Arguably, if post-traumatic growth is just an illusion, I would rather have that illusion than feelings of no progress or hope. Sometimes a placebo effect does work.

How to Have a Hopeful View of Life

Surviving trauma does not necessarily promise a more positive mindset, but a survivor can bounce back from grave disappointment. While I have never lived through the kind of trauma my great-grandma suffered, I did bounce back from splitting up with my ex-husband, and he has since become a trusted friend. I want to be a hopeful and resilient person, one who sees the good in people. Those of us with a more hopeful personality type seem to deliberate less and tend to avoid stewing over life's petty annoyances. We may even try to find the humor in situations.

My mother was well practiced at telling me that the world did not notice how I pined for what could have been or might be in the future. She had no sympathy. No, the world did not rotate around me; she was sure of it. Of course, my sister always added, "Hey, sis, the world just doesn't care. Get over it." This may have been hard to hear earlier in life, but I have taken this to heart. It actually helps me cope, even now.

Resilience and hopeful thinking are useful in combatting the brain's tendency to stick to negativity, and there are ways to nurture hopeful thinking and resilience. One strategy is cognitive reappraisal, a technique used in cognitive behavioral and dialectical behavior therapies, among others. This entails reinterpreting an event or situation, which may take expanding a viewpoint; such reframing may lead a person to more rational thinking. Instead of seeing something in a negative light, we can recalibrate our perspective and give it a hopeful and positive spin. There are ways to deploy this reappraisal.

- Use reflection to help yourself positively reappraise events: "I wasn't so sure about moving to my neighborhood at first, but I made friends and have a wonderful life now."
- Flip the negative into a positive and use reappraisal as a learning tool: "That was a mistake, but here's how I can do better the next time."

How to Be Mentally Agile

Air travel can drive any person mad, and the process can be a nightmare beyond the customary delayed flight. My husband invited his daughter on a vacation to Germany. Her 100-hour-a-week hospital rotations were depleting her, and she needed time away. Plus, his son lived in Berlin. Spending time with both kids would be a double bonus.

Father and daughter proceeded to check in. However, the airline announced that the daughter was not allowed into the country because of pandemic restrictions, even though she was fully vaccinated. They learned that a parent of a German resident was permitted entry, as well as children who were minors, but not an adult sister. Why did the German airline even sell her that ticket in the first place? This thought alone would have made me hopping mad and clouded my mind from thinking straight.

They spent the next hours on the phone calmly canceling their reservations and searching for flights and accommodations in other locations. They boarded a plane to Puerto Rico and had an enjoyable week in balmy weather. Father would have to see his son later in the year. This type of agile thinking halts heated emotional reactions that lead to feeling overwhelmed and paralyzed. Essentially, strong emotions restrict the brain from problem-solving, but an agile thinker can brainstorm solutions.

The idea of this kind of go-with-the-flow unflappability can be found in many areas of therapeutic inquiry, including Gestalt, cognitive behavioral therapy, and acceptance and commitment therapy. Psychologist Steven Hayes, a professor of psychology at the University of Nevada and originator of acceptance and commitment therapy, has examined this ability. As the author of *Get Out of Your Mind and Into Your Life: The New Acceptance and Commitment Therapy*, Hayes may be a bit Buddhist.

Hayes and his colleagues derived the Acceptance and Action Questionnaire, which measures just how mentally rigid a person can be, and they determined that a rigid person has the following negative tendencies:

- Ruminates more and can get stuck in pessimistic loops.
- Feels more anxious.
- Feels more depressed.
- Fears failure and success.

- Seeks perfection.
- Seeks approval from others.
- Suffers more mental health conditions, including mood disorders and beyond.
- Suffers an inability to learn, be curious, or open and relies on habitual responses.
- Cannot expand or grow with new experiences.
- Falls into self-sabotaging behaviors, such as substance abuse, eating disorders, and procrastination.

By contrast, an emotionally agile and flexible person adapts to whatever a situation might call for. He balances different needs in different domains of life by making conscious choices about the time and energy spent on work, home, health, and other areas. He reshapes his mental resources and accesses different perspectives by observing his thoughts and feelings without getting entangled in unhelpful thinking patterns. This person is light on his feet and is adaptive, rather than maladaptive, because he realizes thoughts and feelings are not an accurate reflection of reality, which allows a more flexible view of life situations. He is resilient and doesn't buckle in the face of adversity by engaging in self-compassion, which builds inner strength. He is broad-minded and does not use one tool or method to get through life but tests different strategies and gathers information on what works or doesn't work.

Nurture a Present-Moment Awareness

At the root of a healthy and flexible outlook is being present in the here and now with acceptance and mindfulness. To do this, we can become more aware of ourselves, and a place to start is with the mind and body. When eating an apple, for example, we can bite into the fruit without distractions or thoughts. We focus on the food with all our senses—touch, smell, taste, and hearing. We do not attend to anything but the apple. We can also apply this mindful approach to everyday living by actively listening when a loved one is speaking or looking around us while walking under the trees, or simply taking a deep breath and exhaling slowly.

If we can manage our thoughts and emotions with present-moment awareness, we may better attain what we want in life—the things we value and are dear to us. When we get mired inside our heads about slights, annoyances, grievances, fears, criticisms, insults, or whatever gloom we glom onto, we are not paying attention to what matters. We forget what is meaningful. Ruminating on a negative thought can take us away from truly engaging with the things that are vital to us, what we value.

Here's an example of what I mean. Your child asks you why the sky is blue. You want to be the best parent you can be, but you're not fully engaged with him because you're thinking about a criticism leveled at you during the workday. In this half-state, you're not likely to address your work life in a useful manner, nor will you be the parent you want to be. In effect, you're not getting much done or remembering what is meaningful.

A mentally healthy individual can regulate his emotions and adjust them to whatever his surroundings demand. In research conducted by George Bonanno, a professor of psychology at Columbia University and the author of *The Other Side of Sadness*, people who could modulate their facial expressions while looking at emotion-filled images had better mental health than those who could not.

Showing our emotions is part of everyday social interaction.

When a friend tells us she met someone special, we should show her our interest and enthusiasm. According to Bonnano and his colleague Charles Burton, a research scientist at Yale University, we must, sometimes, show more or less emotion than we feel. Bonnano and Burton developed the Flexible Regulation of Emotional Expression Scale in 2016; this scale measures expressive flexibility. Items on the scale include:

You receive a gift from a family member, but it's a shirt you dislike. *You have to show happy enthusiasm.*

You're attending the funeral of someone you don't know. *You have to be somber.*

You're a guest at a solemn religious ceremony, and the person sitting next to you just whispered a funny joke. *You have to stifle your laughter.*

Researchers, including Bonanno and Burton, have learned that people who regulate their emotions can quickly analyze new information because they can pull back and think rationally. This ability enables a person to see open possibilities in front of them and adapt to new situations. It also helps a person to set aside their knee-jerk reactions and solve problems that come up. People who can regulate how they feel generally have better relationships, romantic, professional, and otherwise.

The Practice of Eating the Bitter

In my younger years, I heard my parents often say *chi ku* (吃苦), which means "eat bitter." They meant that, sometimes, we must endure hard work, pain, and agony to build resilience and reach a goal. In my teens, whenever I complained about homework (usually a chemistry problem), my parents often would say I had to "eat bitter" and push through the difficult tasks. This was their form of tough love. Of course, I'd prefer eating a bowl of ice cream over eating bitter. I often went to my sister for clarification and support; I asked her if they really meant bittersweet. She shook her head and said, "There's nothing sweet here, honey. Only the bitter." According to this mode of thinking, life requires many doses of bitterness. At the core of eating bitter, one must embrace humility, be selfless, and respect others.

Imagine *not* being sad while grieving over a loved one's death. You will only deny what is true. Imagine *not* getting angry over inequality. Sometimes, we need to be angry to take action constructively and productively; progress cannot be made if we sit idly on our hands. Nurturing a psychologically unflappable and flexible mind can help, and there are ways to do this:

- Be mindful and stay in the present to look at what you're feeling: *Why is my heart pounding? I will sit with this feeling to see what is behind my reaction.*
- Avoid being consumed by your thoughts: *I can label my feelings to reduce their intensity.*
- Be a little Buddhist by separating your thoughts from yourself: *I realize that this thought is passing through and not permanent.*
- Look at anxiety and other emotions with objectivity: *I can remember the outcome of similar worries, and I realize that my anxiety was not called for.*
- Examine your feelings without penalty: *I will observe with curiosity and not judge how I feel.*
- Know what you value and stay true to those values: *I know what matters in my life. My family and loved ones are most important.*

My niece was a little girl when she sat beside the master calligrapher Mohamed Zakariya in an Arlington diner. She pointed at his tattoos and asked, "Uncle, what are these?" (It's a Hui custom to address all friends of the family accordingly.)

"I was a bad boy," the artist smiled. "Very bad." When he was young, he got into fistfights. He drifted. Then he trekked to Morocco, a place that lit a fire in him. In the Middle East, he learned about religion, culture, and the meaning of life. He discovered that his life could have a purpose. Knowing your purpose can change everything.

An autodidact by nature, Zakariya taught himself Arabic and carved calligraphy pens to experiment with his newfound passion—all of which may seem strange because he is a very white guy.

Zakariya is now one of the world's living masters in Arabic calligraphy, according to Massumeh Farhad, a curator of Islamic art at the Smithsonian's National Museum of Asian Art. His work has been displayed across the world, and he was even commissioned to create the US postal stamp commemorating the Muslim holiday Eid, as well as a gift for King Abdullah of Saudi Arabia commissioned by President Barack Obama. Zakariya set goals and he reached them. However wild and bumpy his journey to distinction was, he did it because he had a solid growth mindset.

Carol Dweck, a professor of psychology at Stanford University and the author of *Mindset: How You Can Fulfill Your Potential*, developed the idea of the *growth mindset* and the *fixed mindset*. People who feel that talent is innate, and that they cannot change what is inherent, may have a fixed mindset. Those predisposed toward a growth mindset feel they can learn and grow by working hard, thinking strategically, being open to ideas, and collaborating with others. People who want to grow know that everyone has both merits and shortcomings. These types of people aim to improve themselves and are more likely to persist in pursuit of their goals. They know that reaching what they want does take effort.

Grounded in an Upward Mindset

The mindset theory has been explored by many researchers aside from Dweck. Of course, as with any theory, there have been mixed results. In one study of grade-school students appearing in the *Journal of Experimental Psychology*, having a growth mindset did not improve outcomes across the board. This positive mindset seemed to help students who were *already* doing well, while mediocre students did not necessarily improve. Perhaps some students who are already ahead think they can improve even more—as in, success builds upon success. This particular study doesn't mean the mindset theory is not useful, however. As Dweck has noted in her work, people can be a mixture of different mindsets.

In essence, a person can quickly go from a growth to a fixed mindset just by feeling insecure or defensive when others are critical, or when a challenge feels insurmountable. A fixed mindset can close a person to feedback, cooperation, or owning up to mistakes. In effect, growth can get stifled when we feel vulnerable or shut off. This may also lead to the fear of making mistakes. We will not try new things and want to avoid failure and criticism. This is the nature of closed-mindedness and fixed thinking.

Conversely, the growth mindset sees mistakes and failures as opportunities for learning, and criticism as constructive feedback, not personal attacks. People with a growth mindset embrace imperfection and feel it's fine to be flawed and altogether average. For them, engaging in the process is more important than the outcome. For them, being knee-deep in an undertaking is the whole point. They do not have to rush or be the first to finish. Instead, they take their time and are okay with their slow but steady progress.

Attitude and positive thinking certainly help, and the words we use make a difference in how we view learning, growing, and thinking. If we cling to defeatist words (*Why do I even try? I cannot win*), we will not likely push through the obstacles in life. It's not a way to learn from lessons that can be instructive and can help us move toward our goals and objectives.

My father was a good example of someone with a healthy growth mindset and resilience. In his youth, he discovered he was good at studying and test-taking. When various wealthy families in the neighborhood heard about this, they ordered him to take exams for their sons. Dad agreed to do this to avoid a broken nose and being beaten up. At the root of Dad's success was his curiosity. He taught himself to do many things. He learned, through reading, how to ride a horse, shoot a gun, play the harmonica, and swim. Meanwhile, Dad kept attending school, which annoyed his father, who said, "Books are a lofty waste of time and money." His father did not like the idea of higher education; therefore, Dad had to forge his own plan.

He told his father that he would be escorting a few students to a university some three weeks away by foot when he was really escorting *himself* and not coming back. He walked for weeks in a pair of borrowed shoes. To rest his weary feet, he would stop along the side of the road to brew some tea and eat some bread.

To earn money for the tea and bread, he hung a handmade sign that read: ACCOUNTING AND LETTER WRITING WHILE YOU REST. Every few days, he sat on a rock with a calligrapher's brush, ink, paper, and an abacus and had no shortage of patrons. Dad had a lot of gumption, conviction, and burning desires that could not be thwarted. The obstacles were many, including the Japanese War and his unsupportive family. When he finally arrived at the university, he was told that the school had closed because of the bombing, but if he walked three weeks west, there was a school that was still running. And so he kept walking.

How to Nurture Passion and Zeal

Wouldn't it be wonderful if we were all as passionate about our endeavors as my dad? He had the conviction to plug on—walking for weeks and weeks in a borrowed pair of shoes made from hemp. Imagine what we could accomplish with this sort of zeal and enthusiasm.

How do you get fired up and stay fired up? They say you should do what you love, but that was not the case for Dad. He had planned to get a degree in engineering at the first university. Instead, he earned a degree in animal science, the equivalent of veterinary studies, at the second university. It almost didn't matter what he studied, as long as it was something useful, something that would help others, something to help him grow. While Dad had to sweat for his pursuits, he was also a fluid thinker, ready to pivot whenever a situation required. He may have had multiple obstacles in his way, but he also found alternative paths to reach his end goal—of course, that goal kept changing in reality. This kind of fleet-footedness gives hope a chance.

The late psychologist Rick Snyder studied hope, the pursuit of goals, and a diversified perspective and found that a nimble sensibility can help bypass closed doors and see the open ones nearby.

Most people are stuck in the way they think. Yet it doesn't start that way. Little children happily engage in unrestricted thinking. Alison Gopnik, a professor of psychology at the University of California, Berkeley and the author of many books, including *The Scientist in the Crib*, has studied the innate cognitive abilities of children. In one study, she showed adults and children a toy that played music, and everyone was taught how to turn it on by using a set of blocks. The next part of the study entailed turning on the toy with a different set of blocks. The adults mindlessly stuck to their earlier directions, while the children readily discarded prior methods to try new ways to make the toy work.

If we believe our abilities are fixed and go nowhere, they are immutable. If we believe we are capable of moving ahead, then we may just move ahead. Our dedication, curiosity, hard work, and positive outlook may lead us to success. A person with a growth mindset:

- Puts in the effort to master endeavors.
- Learns and grows from their mistakes.
- Sees challenges and setbacks as opportunities.
- Believes that feedback is good.
- Learns and takes inspiration from others.

Be Open-Minded and You Can Make Luck Happen

Traits like hopefulness and a growth mindset are similar to coping strategies like resilience and flexible thinking. They help us be more open to life's potential. The same can be said for the phenomenon of luck. Luck can be just as useful in the quest for positivity. Lucky people are flexible, hopeful, resilient, and open; they mine new opportunities for their own gain and have their eyes peeled for fortune and happy accidents around every corner. Can we learn to be more open to luck?

From their youth, my parents remembered villagers in their homeland panning for gold in a nearby river. Those who panned and hit the jackpot were considered the town's luckiest. A neighbor was one such charmed soul. He had been walking by the river when he stopped for a gulp of water. While on his knees, he saw a glint that begged for a closer look. A rock covered most of that shiny something, so the neighbor lifted the rock and found several gold nuggets, apparently each the size of his thumb. He pocketed these precious lumps and ran home. He didn't squander away the gold on frivolous material goods. Instead, his windfall afforded him and his kin a house, half a mountain, chickens, and goats. He was so lucky.

Luck sticks to certain people, while it doesn't stick to others. The inherently unlucky seem to walk around inviting misfortune. It makes me wonder why this is so. What's more, kismet keeps finding the lucky ones again and again. I like to think that the lucky ones are open and broad-minded. We make our own luck, argues Richard Wiseman, a professor of psychology at the University of Hertfordshire in the United Kingdom and author of *The Luck Factor*. He proposes that we can learn to be curious and lucky in different ways—creating opportunities, feeling lucky, expecting luck to appear wherever and whenever, and seeing the good in the bad. In truth, the lucky are mindful, tolerant, and aware of life's possibilities. Essentially, the lucky are not mired in negative thinking.

Wiseman reports that those who invite this sort of good karma are skilled at moving on to the next thing when fortune is not showing itself. Sometimes you can't get that dream job because someone else occupies the seat; therefore, a mental pivot may be required.

Plus, he says, people open to fortune are also open to risk, this is a useful trait if you want to experience life more fully. There is an *I Can Win* quality to their demeanor. Meanwhile, the unlucky often lament how life offers them no miracles of positive karma. Wiseman noted that those who feel cursed, like the person who thinks he is never given a leg up, create a pattern of self-fulfilling prophecies. You think something will happen and it will happen—as in "I'm not lucky and I never will be."

Quite possibly, people who experience luck early in life expect and look for open doors. Meanwhile, those who do not experience early good karma don't know any better. To put it simply, good tidings beget future good tidings. This is similar to "The Matthew Effect," which was a term coined in the late 1960s by sociologists Robert Merton and Harriet Zuckerman. The phenomenon is named after the Bible's "Parable of the Talents" or Minas in the Gospel of Matthew. This concept acknowledges the advantages of people who are born with more resources. In simple terms, the rich stay rich, so to speak. This also subtly applies to the phenomenon of luck. The lucky stay lucky—or at least they think that way.

A Most Amazing Story of Kismet

The most amazing story of luck I know of involves my parents during the coming of the Chinese Communist Revolution. When Mao Zedong's revolution marched toward their province in the mid-twentieth century, the people were frantic. The wealthy and educated tried to flee the country.

My dad could not secure passage out of the country, but he was educated and worked for the Nationalist Party of China, so he was in danger. At the very least, my dad was determined to get his family (my mom and my older siblings) on the plane, which he did. His family took the last seats, and he was left behind.

As an English speaker, he was often called upon to translate for visiting foreigners. One was Lieutenant General Claire Lee Chennault, the founder of the Flying Tigers, the First American Volunteer Group of the Republic of China Air Force. My dad had helped Chennault negotiate to have an airstrip built in our hometown.

Chennault said to him, "If the Communists catch you, you're a dead man" and told my dad to hide in a pile of lamb's wool and wait. He hid for three days until Chennault ordered an incoming pilot to whisk Dad away.

What luck.

Meanwhile, my mother thought that she would never see him again and that he would surely die in China. After she and her family arrived in Guangdong, she was puffy-eyed and grief-stricken as she sat on a bench with her mother (who secured her own passage), watching refugees moving in and out of an elevator. When the elevator door opened and closed, she was sure she had glimpsed her husband, who was taller than the average Chinese male at nearly six feet in height.

"I think I just saw my husband," she said as she tugged Grandma's sleeve.

Grandma shook her head and said, "You're crying so much that you're seeing things now."

A few minutes later, the elevator opened again, and out walked Dad.

This may be one of the best stories about luck for me. I think Dad was lucky because he believed he was, making him open to looking around and seeing life's possibilities. I want to be lucky like him.

Superstition Can Be a Little Like Luck

A study that appeared in the journal *Psychological Science*, reported that activating superstition, such as carrying a rabbit's foot charm or throwing salt over the shoulder, can boost confidence and performance.

Paul Rozin, a professor of psychology at the University of Pennsylvania and former editor of the research journal *Appetite*, has researched the topic of germs and contagions. He and his colleagues found that people were not amenable to wearing a piece of clothing that had been worn by a murderer, even if it was laundered. The opposite can also be true: When a fan's item of clothing has been touched, and blessed, by his favorite celebrity, he would be hard-pressed to launder the item. Rozin found that people are generally superstitious.

Superstition and luck are related, though people probably interpret these two phenomena in different ways. Superstition is the coalescence of disparate events that happen at the same time, which is why we think it's bad luck when we break a mirror, see a black cat, or walk under a ladder.

My mother was superstitious *all* her life. We would clean and dust the house each Thursday. After that, we could welcome dead ancestors into our home. On Friday afternoons, Mom would place sticks of incense in a cup of sand and get on her knees to pray to kin who had passed. She would ask them for forgiveness as well as ask for advice for fixing any wrongness. I surmise that this action made her feel better. It made her feel hopeful, and there is nothing wrong with hope.

I have my own ritual of always wearing a headscarf when we visit the graves of our loved ones. In the grand scheme, I don't abide by my mother's rituals and rules, and I shouldn't have to fake my way with a headscarf. Yet I stand on the soil wearing the scarf anyway. In truth, I feel comfortable embracing my personal spirituality, especially if I am under a tree. It's also a reminder of who I am—in sneakers and a scarf.

When We're Open to the Possibilities

We can find opportunities if we are open to them. However, we could be open to seeing what is in front of us. When we are open, we can make use of a chance situation. This ability bolsters our confidence and the potential to take risks, helping us see possibilities in unlikely places. That's the way opportunity works.

Flexibility of mind means openness, and it helps all life situations. If you are flexible, you are open to anything that may come under your purview.

To cultivate this capacity:

- Try new things, eat different foods, and go to new places.
- Even if you're a little uncomfortable, talk to someone new.
- Ask questions and listen to opposing points of view.
- Refrain from judging others—these people may end up being a colleague, a friend, or even a mate.

Such flexibility keeps us from being emotionally charged. When we are distraught, we become immobilized and have difficulty thinking more rationally. This ability to be flexible means being less rigid and more adaptable, which promotes better emotion regulation. This can nurture a growth mindset that allows curiosity and learning. People with this mindset do not avoid failure or criticism; they keep plugging away in the spirit of inquiry.

Likewise, resilience and hopeful thinking are also useful in combatting the brain's tendency for negativity. Resilience helps us face fears, reframe our viewpoint, problem-solve, be open, focus on what can happen and what can be done, and other positive behaviors. Generally, hopeful thinking and resilience protect us when we feel beleaguered from life.

These positive coping strategies can also be nurtured through cognitive reappraisal and reinterpreting an event or situation. This may reframe our perspective and give a situation a more optimistic view. With this view, we might give life a more positive spin.

Chapter Six

You Don't Have to Sit in Loneliness

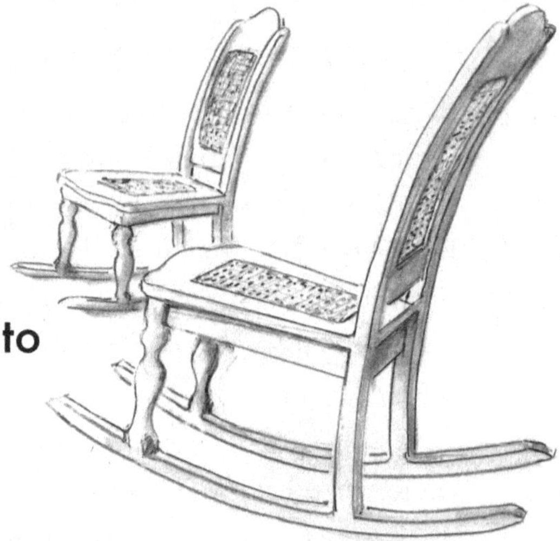

I've had three distinct periods in my life when loneliness was an underlying theme: during my teenage years, at the start of college, and when I got divorced in my late thirties. That first episode felt oddly detached. Life seemed filled with work—schoolwork, homework, plus endless chores my mom made up. What was the point? The second came because I had no idea what I was supposed to be doing at college. The last episode happened when my first husband left. Even though I had small kids under my charge, I don't remember much at all except the feeling of drifting like a ghost, not dead but not alive either.

My Hui family network in Qinghai ensures that isolation is always kept in check. They do not allow network members to slip into the abyss of loneliness. You can expect that loved ones will be, in effect, always in your face. If they knock on your door, you must answer whether you want to or not. They will barge in with buns and bread, hovering over you to surmise the exact symptoms you suffer.

Are you physically ill? If so, they threaten to hail the doctor or haul you to the clinic. If there are no outward physical indicators, they will move on to other possible ailments—including emotional ones. While one cousin pinpoints the symptoms, another cousin charges into your kitchen to make tea and then forces you to drink. If you look like you're not on the verge of vomiting, they move on to soup and buns.

This kind of intervention may seem over the top, but loneliness is real and requires real attention.

My family would have helped me more during my periods of isolation, but proximity was a problem. Everyone was spread across the US; it is so much easier when people are closer to each other. Fortunately, I have made friends with neighbors and work colleagues. When a neighbor had a virus that kept her in bed for days, I brought over bottled water. This, along with my check-up texts, were small gestures on my part, but it meant a lot to her. She later said she didn't feel so alone.

We all feel lonely now and then. It's part of life. Yet health officials have deemed loneliness a real national health crisis. More than half of Americans have felt isolated at one time or another, according to a 2018 Cigna Health survey of more than ten thousand people. The number of 58 percent may sound high, but many people experience loneliness even while in the company of others. People in relationships can suffer a certain degree of emptiness, especially if their union is unhappy.

Young people, as well as the very elderly, suffer the most. The young, who are surrounded by extensive digital networks and numerous social media contacts, can still feel cut off and emotionally rudderless, and those with fewer but closer relationships may be better insulated. Younger people, aged eighteen to twenty-four, are twice as likely to be more lonely than older adults aged sixty-six and older.

The Health Risks of Isolation

Isolation that remains unmonitored can lead to serious health problems, including a higher risk of heart disease, cognitive decline, type 2 diabetes, and suicidal thoughts. It can even lower immunity. Loneliness is stressful; therefore the body releases cortisol. This hormone is useful in small doses—cortisol alerts you to danger if you're in a dark and unfamiliar alley, for example. But if your body produces this hormone chronically, your cardiovascular and immune systems are thrown out of whack. According to the American Psychological Association, in recent years, some half of adults report being negatively affected by stress in general.

Stress can also increase inflammation, which is equally harmful. Again, in measured doses, inflammation is protective. In the case of skin swelling around a cut, for instance, blood flow to the injury or infection is good. However, chronic immune system activation is not healthy as inflammation can damage cells and tissues.

Research from the American Psychological Association has found that when fighting the simple common cold, lonely people suffer more symptoms than the non-lonely. Loneliness increases the risk of disease overall. There is also a link between social pain and the physical pain of isolation. The journal *Annals of Behavioral Medicine* reported research in 2019 showing that a course of everyday pain relievers, such as acetaminophen or ibuprofen, can ease the emotional aches of loneliness.

For counteracting loneliness, we should all be more like my husband, who dives into whatever he finds interesting. Once, while I was away visiting my mom for a week, he took up kiteboarding. Over the years, he has met a robust network of people who have become his close friends. I have benefitted and made friends through this network, too.

If we don't want to learn kiteboarding, we can extend ourselves by:

- Reaching out to a friend. Even if she seldom reaches out, the connection has to start somewhere.
- Volunteering. I joined an environmental clean-up group, and it is one of the best decisions I have made. I help clean the environment and I make friends.
- Playing sports. A friend of mine started playing pickleball and swears by this method of making new friends.
- Joining a spiritual group. Another friend created a Bible study group twenty years ago, and it is still going strong.
- Joining a parenting group. You can actually meet people at the PTA.
- Continuing your education. My local library has events like crafting, meditation groups, art history lectures, and more.
- Making friends at work. I have made many friends through various workplaces, and we keep in touch.

The Difference Between Loneliness and Solitude

While solitude sounds similar to loneliness, the two states of being are decidedly not the same. We could all use a lesson from my grandpa. He was a mountain man who coveted his solitude. He traveled the high plateaus above the Gobi Desert as a trader hawking thread, shoes, tea, and even bullets, and was often away for weeks at a time, walking with his donkey piled with wares. He preferred the fresh air and his four-legged ride over the chatter of people, who demanded his time and money.

People who seek the quiet embrace of being in their own company don't feel lonely. The person who yearns for solitude is perfectly content as a hermit in self-imposed seclusion. Therefore, being alone may be a matter of perception for some of us. We do not choose loneliness, but we do choose solitude.

The words "monk" and "monastic" are derived from the Greek term *monos* or alone. The monk sequesters himself in solitude to find inner peace by meditating and not speaking. He shuns the buzz of distraction to find himself. Likewise, many artists seek this peace and silence and connect with themselves. My brother hikes in the Sierras and prefers to be alone with his drawing pad and pencils. He spends time in nature, looking for motivation and inspiration.

Researcher Bella DePaulo, affiliated with the University of California, Santa Barbara and the author of *Single at Heart: The Power, Freedom, and Heart-Filling Joy of Single Life*, has thought thoroughly about what it means to be alone. She studied whether we should worry about what other people think when they see us alone; she found that the answer was *no*. She and her colleagues came to this conclusion after editing photographs of people dining in restaurants either in a group, as part of a couple, with a friend, or sitting alone. She then showed these doctored images to study participants, and they did not think the people who dined alone were losers.

Being in solitude does not mean being socially isolated. To learn how to be alone now and then, we can be at ease when we are on our own, and we can leave our phones behind. When we are alone, we can let the mind wander about happy moments, not about our anxieties or defeatist ruminations. If we sit under a tree and listen to the stillness, we may develop a better idea of who we are.

Why Relationships Are Important

While it's good to have moments of solitude, it's also good to have a reliable network of friends. I came across a study from the Association of Psychological Science about the relationship between friendship and proximity. In the study, the findings showed that among students who sat in randomly assigned seats, those sitting next to each other had higher ratings of friendship intensity one year later, and the same was true even if the students sat in the same row.

This makes a lot of sense. I make friends with my neighbors. On Sunday mornings, we sometimes simply text each other, "Tea?" This time with friends also works like free therapy sessions, during which we can relay the week's highlights and touch upon what's going on with family, work, and love.

Sharing a cup of tea and a steamed bun with friends was a ritual during my grandparents' time. I hope I'm still surrounded by friends when I'm well into old age. Focusing on others pulls me out of myself, and I read that having this type of support can also improve cognition and help prevent dementia. One 2008 study, from the *American Journal of Public Health*, shows that elderly women with stronger social networks were less likely to develop cognitive decline. If I were to lose my mind, I would want my friends around.

George Vaillant, a principal investigator of Harvard Medical School's landmark Grant Study of Adult Development, came to a solid conclusion: What matters the most in life is our relationships with other people—partners, loved ones, work colleagues, and others. This study of only men found that those who enjoyed warm relationships, particularly with their mothers, earned more, while those who shared warm relationships with their fathers suffered less anxiety.

But it takes time and investment to make a friend, as well as curiosity and open-minded thinking. In a study published in 2018 in the *Journal of Social and Personal Relationships*, in order to turn an acquaintance into more than just an acquaintance, you need about 50 hours of interaction. Beyond that, roughly 90 hours are needed to turn a part-time friend into a true friend. If you're looking for a bestie, you may need to interact for more than 200 hours.

A person can break out of their unhappy mental loops by making friendship a priority and maintaining those bonds at every stage of life.

Don't Spread Negativity in Relationships

Yet goodwill and connection are hard to come by, and human relations have taken a dark turn. Civility has lost its way in our public discourse. The global communication and engagement firm Weber Shandwick reported that 93 percent of Americans say this nation has a civility problem, with 69 percent saying incivility has become a major concern. Considering our brain's tendency toward the negative, we notice misery and rude behavior more than kindness, and misery can easily spread from one person to another. A rude person can be compassionless, intractable, and stubborn—all of which compounds the negativity we collectively suffer. Politicians and talking heads shout obscenities while trolls and shamers infiltrate all corners of the Internet. This caustic and impolite discourse even trickles into households and work cubicles.

There are some things to think about:

- Negativity can spill into our daily interactions.
- It can start a chain reaction of misery.
- If negativity is tolerated in a group, the emotion is more likely to multiply.
- We can counter this by rejecting it and spreading our positivity instead.

I have heard a daughter in our neighborhood shouting at her mom, "I'm talking on the phone, not to you." Or a parent shouting to their child, "I wish you were never born." These distressing child-parent interactions are not uncommon.

I have an aunt who, at the slightest glimpse of offspring discourtesy, had said to her daughter, "Be polite to me." The daughter's arms and legs moved in painful contortions while she replied, "I Am Trying to Be Polite to You." Each word seemed excruciating for her to say.

If we spread goodwill and positivity, we may be less inclined to get caught up in a cycle of pessimism. It has to start in our homes and workplaces. My Hui elders like to remind the rest of us that one must always respect and do the right thing for the elderly, the sick, and the orphaned. No matter what, you must oblige others with kindness. Honoring family and respecting our fellow humans makes for a better world.

Share Your Bowl of Noodles

A term in my home dialect tries to explain the experience of loved ones gathering together. It is *rey noh*, (热脑), which means "warm brain." It's that warm and fuzzy feeling of being with loved ones. Of course, food is always served to facilitate the warm and fuzzy feeling.

Food is the main attraction for most cultures, and warm brain is usually the result. Many studies show that sitting down for a family meal has many benefits. Among these studies, one in the *Archives of Pediatrics and Adolescent Medicine* showed that eating together enhances the health and well-being of adolescents. On the other hand, people who suffer from eating disorders or other mental health difficulties tend to eat alone.

In modern-day America, many of us eat at our desks while looking at screens. Productivity is key. And at home, many of us eat in front of a blaring TV. A 2022 report in the journal *Appetite* found that we eat a less healthy diet when we eat in front of a screen. In contrast, eating together is essential in many cultures; you cannot eat alone.

When we visited our relatives in Qinghai near the Tibetan plateau, they hosted elaborate banquets. *Rey noh* mandates that the host provide ten courses—braised chicken, fish in sweet sauce, dumplings, artisanal bread, sweet cakes, and so much more. In many cultures, sharing a bowl and *rey noh* is the foundation of life. Sharing food and love gets you out of your head.

On one visit when I was younger, I stood in the courtyard

of a mud-adobe house, marveling over how my dad grew up in this very home. I popped a morsel of warm pan-cooked bread into my mouth, thinking that my dad had eaten the same type of bread. My Uncle Number Three caught me chewing, he looked at me as if I was raised by animals. "Cannot eat standing like this. It's disrespectful to humanity." Then he lectured me on the meaning of a meal, and how we must sit and honor every dish with family and friends. (Older generations are terrific at guilt-tripping younger people.)

Sharing a Bowl with Siblings

I thought my sister was far too bossy when I was younger. I annoyed her by never listening to her advice. Much later, when I finally wised-up, I realized, *Why didn't I take her advice?* It would have saved me *so much* trouble. Finally, I started listening. After my divorce, I was a clueless mother who suffered from a low-grade but persistent depression. With my sister's support, along with that of my brothers and friends, my little raft kept afloat. My sister and I became accustomed to talking every few days, discussing the crucial, as well as the mundane—from worries about our children to the right oven temperature for roasted lamb.

Brothers and sisters have a shared history. They have a bond that does not need articulating. I rely on my siblings. Discord with a sibling is like shooting oneself in any body part. In Hui culture, brothers and sisters who don't get along are subject to losing face; plus gatherings continue even if one brother irritates another. Blood sticks together even if arguing members are not getting along.

Having an emotionally close relationship with a sibling can

mean huge health benefits, such as less depression and higher life satisfaction in one's later years. A 2012 study that was published in the journal *International Sociology* showed that people who have suffered substandard relationships with siblings also suffered hardships in the forms of addiction, financial woes, or poor mental health.

Geoffrey Greif, a professor at the University of Maryland School of Social Work and the author of *Adult Sibling Relationships*, found that siblings can be friends. In a study with 262 adults, 64 percent said they considered at least one of their siblings to be a good friend, and 45 percent said they considered at least one of their siblings to be among their best friends.

Other People Matter

The late Christopher Peterson and Martin Seligman authored the book *Character Strengths and Virtues: A Handbook and Classification* and are known as the forefathers of positive psychology. Peterson was a professor of psychology at the University of Michigan and science director of the VIA Institute on Character, and Seligman is director of the Positive Psychology Center at the University of Pennsylvania. In their research, and the research of others, having positive relationships determines a person's level of health and happiness. Peterson had firmly stated that *other people matter*.

For example, researchers found that caring behaviors release stress-reducing hormones like oxytocin. Known as the "love or cuddle hormone," oxytocin is released into the bloodstream when we engage in social connection. This can happen through physical affection, meaningful eye contact, or emotional bonding, among other things. Oxytocin is similar to other hormones like cortisol and vasopressin, which can induce prosocial connections like empathy, trust, and compassion. Having good relationships means a healthy, happy, and meaningful life.

When we are focused on others, we get out of ourselves—namely out of our heads. Worries, anxieties, and ruminations take a back seat. Why do we feel great after we help others or volunteer our time and efforts? Essentially, altruism activates the pleasure and reward centers in the brain. Called the *helper's high*, the act of being charitable and selfless releases hormones like endorphins, which reduce stress, relieve pain, and improve mood. The benefits also include better cardiovascular health, lower blood pressure, and even a longer life.

When we focus on others, we get outside ourselves and the problems we carry. This outward focus can boost our well-being. Even the act of hoping for another person's happiness releases hormones that boost mood. When Peterson said that *other people matter*, he lived by that creed. He had many people in his life, and they all mattered. I learned from him that the form of these relationships is up to us; family is what we want it to be. I see my friends as lifelong family. They are part of my tribe.

Why You Feel Safe Within Your Tribe and Fight for Your In-Group

During my great-grandparents' time, our Hui people accused the Han people of price-fixing the everyday bamboo pole. Why should one ethnic minority, the out-group, pay more than another? The Hui revolted, and that hate brought the deaths of millions of Han and Hui throughout Middle China. The Hui are an ethnic Muslim out-group like the Uyghur and Sala. One uncle from that time tried to negotiate a treaty with the Han, but the authorities threw him into the town dungeon and sentenced him to death. When he was executed, his head fell to the ground and rolled to his wife's knees. She grabbed his head, and her brothers wrapped his body in white cloth and carried him home, where she stitched his head back onto his body for a proper death.

In evolutionary psychology, your tribe or in-group ensures your survival, protecting you from loneliness and disease. Your in-group also affords you a place in society; it's where you belong. In-groups and out-groups can be described as tribes; there is an *us-versus-them* mentality. In the case of the beheaded uncle, the Hui and the Han hated each other. It was *us* versus *them*. Countless social psychology studies have found that your in-group protects and supports you, and you feel pride because you belong. Everyone needs to belong somewhere.

According to many researchers, including evolutionary psychologist Glenn Geher, when a person is cast from their group, they can feel isolated and vulnerable. After this, ill health—both mental and physical—can take hold. The caveman of prehistoric times didn't last too long outside the safety of his tribe.

A tight-knit, supportive group protects its members from harm. Researchers have found that people identify with their clan more intensely if physically threatened. When someone is hostile to us, our cortisol shoots up, and we look for protection from our in-group. Finding protection within your tribe is an evolutionary action innately programmed within us.

Yet, there is a golden mean for everything. Staying completely inside the confines of your tribe at all times can be harmful. Too much pride in the tribe can morph into feelings of narcissism, which leads us to feel that our clan is better than others. Sports fans often highlight this most violently. How many news stories have we read about fans rioting after a game? After the 2023 NCAA men's basketball championship between the University of Connecticut Huskies and the San Diego State University Aztecs, for example, rioters in Connecticut flipped cars, started fires, and broke into buildings on campus, with sixteen people hospitalized and fifteen people arrested. Hot-blooded tribalism can bring out the worst in us, and this is how hate and negativity hold forth.

We Can Belong Where We Are

The younger me sometimes felt rudderless, like I never belonged anywhere. This mental and physical drifting was likely an underlying concern for my parents and siblings. We had no place, no home, and the ancestral home in Qinghai is no longer ours. I remember that my mom cooked with an air of loneliness like she had lost something important, but I was too young to give her any comfort. Our meal preparation was unlike the kitchens of our homeland where people bustled with humor and solidarity.

We often hear about people who move back to their hometown to raise kids and be close to their kin. However, none of my siblings felt rooted in the East Los Angeles neighborhood of our youth; no one went back after Dad died and Mom moved. My parents missed their faraway kin. Their sense of belonging had been sapped. Children just follow their parents, so my three siblings and I were homeless wanderers as well.

Once in a while, I feel like I was robbed of something important. It's a mixture of missing a part of my youth and never having a sense of community. This gives me a tiny inkling of what my parents must have felt. Many people like my parents have been displaced; in a 2022 global count by the UN Refugee Agency, 35.3 million refugees had fled their countries of origin. Others have lost their homes due to natural disasters like wildfires and hurricanes.

Americans are known for their mobility, whether for work, a better cost of living, or a better school for their children. So it's surprising that 40 percent of Americans live in the town they grew up in. A 2008 Pew Research survey shows that people stay put because of family, especially if there are kin within a reasonable distance.

Science writer Melody Warnick has written in her book *This Is Where You Belong: The Art and Science of Loving the Place You Live* that having a sense of place helps shape your identity, health, happiness, and mental landscape. This is the relationship we have with our surroundings, not to mention the emotions we have about a particular place. This place is unique to us, and it has a distinctive quality because it is important to us. According to Warnick, we can come to love the place where we live and feel at home. We can learn to love where we are.

I have moved around, and I know what she is saying. Trying to settle into a new location is unsettling. It took me many years to feel comfortable in my neighborhood, to make friends, and to feel like I belonged here. To develop place attachment, we can get to know our neighbors and build trust in the people in the community. You can also get to know the physical spaces as well. I go to the duck pond down the street and have a personal attachment to it like it belongs to me. Likewise, there is a nearby café I love that also belongs to me.

People can feel rooted in their town and feel a sense of belonging, and the benefits are valuable—they feel comfort, safety, continuity, and support. A Japanese study showed that people who had an attachment to where they lived had five additional years of longevity when compared with people who had no affinity for their location. A 2011 study in the journal *Developmental Psychology* found that young people who weren't uprooted enjoyed higher levels of well-being.

Beyond the health and well-being effects of loving your community, there are monetary advantages as well. A Gallup and Knight Foundation report showed that the more people felt happy in their community, the better the economy of that community. Plus, if you have friends nearby, you'll enjoy what feels like additional income in your pocket. Friendship is invaluable.

A Dip into Nostalgia

A sense of home and place is a bit like nostalgia. Memories and longing for childhood often feel bittersweet and wistful. My father used the word *xiang* (想), for nostalgia. It's a versatile word that can mean "to think," "want," "wish," "suppose," or "feel like doing." It is also used when remembering or missing something or someone from your past. It's the sensation I got when I watched my eldest son, then a tween, walking through the subway turnstile on his own for the first time.

Psychologist Krystine Batcho of Le Moyne College in Syracuse, New York, thinks nostalgia is like a "mental time machine," where we turn back the clock and travel into the past. This reflection is often viewed from the eyes of childhood. I feel delight when I think of my very first memory, a pair of gold slippers on my feet. We relive the past in a positive way. According to Batcho, nostalgia doesn't trap us in the past; we are just traveling to yesteryear and connecting with ourselves and our loved ones. This recollection includes people, especially ones in important gatherings. Not long ago, we watched a video of my friends getting married about forty years ago. The video made us happy.

This reflection feels good because it triggers hormones like serotonin and dopamine, the same hormones released when we feel joy. Batcho noted that we use the best of our past to rediscover what will continue to be meaningful to us.

Of course, we are picky about what we want to remember regarding the past. Most people don't want to take *every* memory with them, so we want to highlight the good and positive stuff as much as possible. Generally, according to Batcho, we want to be the hero in the story. We want to be the one who controls the narrative, overcoming every obstacle in the way. It reinforces bonds and the feeling of home, family, and belonging; it's a comfortable feeling that sets a person right when things feel slightly wrong. When we long for the good old days, nostalgia may cast a rose-tinted view of the past.

Welcome Others Around You

Our tribe is important, but we should also look outward and be open. We have to see what's going on outside our group. Being open to others and what they have to say can help us in many ways. Sticking only to one's tribe may perpetuate negative stereotypes and hateful attitudes about other people. When we spread goodwill and positivity, it comes back to us.

There are ways to be more open to other people and their views—especially when they are different from us:

- Be empathetic about their circumstances; doing so may encourage our humility.
- Listen without commentary or judgment.

- Find commonality. We may have differences, but we likely have things in common.
- When we show people that they matter, our well-being will benefit.
- This openness may help us be less pessimistic about humanity.
- Being open to other people and their perspectives may even help us stop fighting with each other.

Chapter Seven

The Mindful Relationship

Many of us also want to have a sense of belonging when it comes to love and intimacy, and we may fantasize about and imagine who might be the right match for us. I count myself lucky. My husband is extremely thoughtful. He is accepting of people and is willing to hear what they have to say, especially what *I* have to say. He waits and listens *long* before he opens his mouth. For mindful people like him, an argument is not an argument; it's a discussion with an even-keeled back and forth.

It should not come as a surprise that one of the most desirable elements of a great relationship is mindfulness, which is essential for a positive union. A person who is mindful about her relationship pays attention to her partner without judgment. There is an objective quality when we try to understand our partner's perspective and listen without a predetermined agenda. This foundation is helpful when we try to communicate what is on our minds; it can enable us to communicate and connect with our partners with vulnerability, kindness, gratitude, and support.

This type of thoughtfulness brings harmony. According to research in the journal *American Psychologist*, when discussions are conducted effectively, nearly half of the relationships studied get stronger and 44 percent of even-tempered partners get the respect they deserve. In contrast, when an argument turns into an aggressive fight, 35 percent of relationships weaken and 29 percent of hot-tempered partners lose the respect they want. Partners who cannot recognize the root of their anger feel emotions that are more intense and harder to manage.

When we deconstruct the everyday fights that most married couples experience, it's clear that many of them often start as minor arguments like this:

"Why can't you do the dishes once in a while?"

"I did the dishes yesterday. It's your turn."

If there isn't mindfulness involved, the minor argument may grow into a major one, with one partner resorting to an ugly character assassination such as, "You are so useless." This is how the small task of washing dishes grows into something else.

We Fight the Same Fights Over and Over

Here's another scenario: Partner A wants Partner B to scrub the toilet more often. She can't understand why the lion's share of house chores falls on her. Partner B can withstand a less-tidy home, yet he realizes he *should* pitch in at least once in a while, so he shows up with a scrubbing brush. But a week or two later, he forgets the toilet may need attention—it's always clean anyhow. Partner A becomes incensed that she must nag him about it again. Without mindfulness, this becomes an unresolved pattern. In such a scenario, Partner B might act like the wounded child, and Partner A, the grouchy parent.

Michael Puett, a professor of history and anthropology at Harvard, and education and parenting journalist Christine Gross-Loh have researched how people engage in similar circular debates, and they found that it's useful when both the wounded child and the grumpy parent become aware of their unhealthy patterns of communication. If partners want harmony, both parties have to say what needs to be said thoughtfully, and both parties have to make the effort to listen.

To do this, we can use active listening, a therapeutic technique deployed in many therapy types from cognitive behavioral therapy to person-centered therapy. Active listening means *really* hearing what is being said. We have to look at our partner face to face, repeat what is being said, come at the information from their perspective, and ask questions with genuine and objective interest. This may help us better understand our partner.

One common problem is that people get stuck and mentally sidetracked by other matters that bother them, and they aren't truly listening to each other about the topic of discussion. Their minds may roll over and over with negative thoughts about everything wrong in their relationship, with past grudges and other unsettled disputes coming to the forefront.

When partners are in an intense and emotionally laden "we need to talk" talk, it can quickly become an endless, unstructured debate about their many tangential points of contention. Partners can benefit just by being alert to *how* they converse. We can listen objectively by focusing on the tone of our partner's message. Does the person sound strained or relaxed? We can also objectively observe the nonverbal expressions they use. Does the person pace the floor, or are they sitting comfortably?

How to Use Emotion Regulation to Get Along

Neuroscientist Eric Haseltine, a former intelligence officer with the National Security Agency and former executive with Walt Disney Imagineering, spent time earlier in his career counseling violent men. These were men who felt trapped by and hopeless about their aggression. When they were being hotheaded, their overriding thought was, "That isn't me." Deep down, they did not want to harm anyone.

Haseltine used a two-step process to get through to these aggressive men. In the first step, he suggested that the men get in touch with their feelings through physical awareness. If, for example, a tight chest and a clenched fist were signs they were about to get aggressive, Haseltine said this was the cue for getting up and leaving the situation. This process comes from treatments such as cognitive behavioral therapy, which entails replacing negative behavior with productive behavior repeatedly.

There is also a tendency for many of us to assign blame in the middle of a conversation. Ours is a culture that looks for someone to blame. Social psychologist Susan Krauss Whitbourne, professor emerita at the University of Massachusetts Amherst and the author of *The Search for Fulfillment: Revolutionary New Research That Reveals the Secret to Long-Term Happiness*, thinks blame comes in two forms: We instantly find the next person responsible, or we always point the finger at the mirror. "Some people are never responsible for *anything*, and others always feel responsible for *everything*," she says.

Blaming others is a common defense mechanism to protect oneself from guilt and shame. People who cannot deal with their emotions would rather place responsibility on others. Conversely, self-blame may be a survival strategy that allows a person to feel some sort of control over situations. Blaming oneself can happen after a mishap: *It's my fault that my partner forgot to take his medication.*

Essentially, blame can sabotage us and our relationships. The infractions and slights that we mull over have a cost. This type of thinking ends up consuming our thoughts. For some, when things seem wrong in life, it's easiest to look at other people: "Why is my life so difficult? Maybe my life would be better if I weren't married to this person. Maybe she's the real problem." It's easy to point fingers. We are often hardest on our closest relations because they are the ones who are more likely to forgive our transgressions. Like the saying goes, we only hurt the ones we love.

How to Change Our Behavior

The evidence-based approach of behavioral activation is used with patients feeling depression and deep distress. It is a technique used in cognitive behavioral therapy, among other therapies, and can be deployed outside of therapy as well. A person's activity level can be activated to pull them out of their heads. The idea is to engage in what is meaningful to us, whether it's showing gratitude toward a loved one, walking in nature, practicing yoga, or any number of things that make us feel we have a life worth living. There are few ways to activate ourselves out of negativity:

- Setting small, attainable goals: *I will go for a walk to clear my head.*

- Scheduling routines that show appreciation toward our partners: *I will make coffee and take it to my partner.*
- Combatting negativity by questioning the negative thoughts and feelings that come up: *Why am I fixated on my partner's comment?*
- Asking what it is that we're avoiding: *Am I delaying because I fear something?*

We Can't Change Other People

People who are unhappy with their own lives often project everything wrong onto their partners, with the focus on "How can I change my partner?" They may spend a lot of time drifting back to past arguments and grievances where, in their minds, the partner remains guilty on all counts. Then their emotions bubble up and take over, and they react to their feelings without examining what is happening. It's more helpful to inspect our thoughts and emotions for information. For example:

"What is my anger telling me right now?"

"What am I afraid of?"

"What am I avoiding?"

Wading around in pessimistic thoughts about a relationship is easy—especially when we feel hurt or attacked by our partner. But partners should focus on how to improve themselves, as well as how they *think* about their relationship.

When we stew about an unsatisfactory exchange we've had with our partner, we might replay events and thoughts that upset us. However, we can instead:

- Recognize when we are ruminating about a negative thought. *I keep thinking about the jab my co-worker made at me in the company-wide meeting.*
- Understand what triggers the thought. *When people elbow me, I feel dumb.*
- Interrupt and dispute the negative thought. *Do I need to dwell on this?*
- Set a boundary with your thoughts. *Thinking about this interaction is getting me nowhere.*
- Problem-solve the thought. *The next time it happens, I will think calmly and ask for the meaning behind the interaction.*

The Michelangelo Effect

Early work on a phenomenon called the "Michelangelo Effect" came from psychologists Stephen Michael Drigotas of Johns Hopkins University and Caryl Rusbult of the Vrije Universiteit in Amsterdam, among other colleagues. Their research appeared in a 1999 *Journal of Personality and Social Psychology* paper titled, "Close Partner as Sculptor of the Ideal Self: Behavioral Affirmation and the Michelangelo Phenomenon." Deploying the Michelangelo Effect can be useful if you want a more mindful partnership. The idea is that each partner can "sculpt" the other into their best self. Aaron Ben-Ze'ev, University of Haifa professor and author of *The Arc of Love: How Our Romantic Lives Change Over Time*, has written about the Michelangelo phenomenon, and he notes that intimate partners can coax each other's ideal selves into reality. It is the trope, "You bring out the best in me." I am fortunate that my husband lets me be me without pestering or pressuring. I also model my behavior after his. When his work project is a winner, I want to win at work, too. When he works out and eats healthy food, I work out and eat healthy food, too.

This idea is related to "confirmation bias," in which you interpret all evidence as confirming your preconceived beliefs. In essence, you say you will do a good job on an upcoming presentation, and therefore you do a good job. This is also related to the concept of self-fulfilling prophecies, where your beliefs and expectations influence how you behave. Beliefs and expectations can affect all areas of life, including relationships. If you believe you will have a harmonious relationship, you will likely do the work to make this happen.

I used to think that other people needed fixing (people were probably thinking the same thing about me). I realize now that my thinking was entirely arrogant. My sister once told me to sort out my own crap before I looked at the way others disappointed me. Oddly, when I started sorting myself out, I stopped feeling let down by others, and the disappointments no longer felt so disappointing. It was as if my deep discontent over the infractions and slights of others had faded. To sort yourself out, you can:

- Try to observe yourself from a distance.
- Think about what keeps you from moving forward.
- Are you stuck on something from your past?
- Address this without ruminating about it.
- Pinpoint what you value in life.
- Your values will be your beacon.

Relationships Take Work

When it comes to unions and marriages, the following thought has been attributed to many people, but whoever said it first was onto something: "Every relationship is the one relationship you should not be in." Sometimes, I feel like I want to divorce myself, and if I cannot be with myself, where does that leave me and my partner? All relationships are challenging.

Relationships take work, and they do not always behave. People do not get everything they expect, want, or desire in their relationships. These are common-sense facts. To keep a relationship strong and healthy, we should deploy a few strategies to maintain it. When we engage in active listening, for example, we do so with openness, respect, trust, and vulnerability in a quiet environment without distractions. We can do so by using *I* statements, which helps put aside blame and defensiveness.

Some commonplace examples may include:

"I feel sad when I finish work and return to an untidy house" instead of "Why is this house always a dump?"

"I feel unheard" instead of "Why do you always interrupt me?"

"I felt awkward when you talked to your co-worker for fifteen minutes" instead of "Why were you flirting with that woman?"

If we want our long-term union to endure, we have to accept the relationship we have, not the one we think we should have. Our expectations may require some adjustment and compromise; in doing so, we may have a better idea of our partner's needs. Needs and desires often change over time, so it's good to routinely check in with each other. It's also easy to take a relationship for granted. Sometimes it helps to see our partners as if they just walked in the door after being away from home for weeks in order to renew our appreciation of them.

If we add kids to the mix, the picture gets *much* more complicated. It's no surprise that children raised in dysfunctional and volatile environments usually don't fare well—such environments can include heated conflict, substance abuse, authoritarian parents who dictate and demand, or neglectful parents who dismiss their child's needs. In a 2018 study published in the *Journal of Personal and Social Relationships*, about one hundred children were given a survey that determined whether they came from low- or high-conflict homes; the children were then divided into these two groups. Both groups were shown photos of couples, some in happy poses, some angry, and some neutral. The researchers found that the children from high-conflict homes were less likely to recognize couples in emotionally neutral poses; they thought that either these couples might be angry or happy, but not neutral. Kids from high-conflict homes could not entirely read people, and this disadvantage could fuel difficulty for them later in life. There are myriad ill effects when someone is raised in an unhappy environment, including depression and anxiety.

If we have kids, we want a better handle on what is happening with them, and this can happen when a couple works together. A while ago, for example, I noticed a striking red headed woman strolling down the hill with her school-age son. At the train station, she handed the boy to a lady I presumed to be the nanny. I later realized the redheaded woman was connected to a handsome tall man, the boy's father. I would see the man sometimes walking a block behind or ahead of the boy's mother. They never walked together. This couple moved around each other like repelling magnets, rarely talking. I thought they were separated, but I didn't know for sure. Then one evening, I saw them walking up the hill together, and he was carrying her bag. This made me smile; if they were separated, they were still working together to raise their child. I admired their cooperation toward a shared goal, the well-being of their child.

The Desperation of a Bad Relationship

Unhappy relationships fuel desperation, negativity, and lots of mindlessness. People often engage in revisionist history when a relationship nears its end. It's easy to see a union as something bad, especially as it's dissolving. We do this to protect ourselves and the decisions we make. We may tell ourselves, "She was wrong for me." "It wasn't meant to be." Or, "I knew it all along." We are often closed-minded in our thoughts and behaviors when relationships evaporate into nothingness.

But it doesn't have to be that way. Fortunately, my ex-husband was fully aware of how conflict can shatter lives and affect children; we both tried to keep the acrimony at bay as we dissolved our marriage. Researchers including the late Constance Ahrons, a professor at the University of Southern California and the author of the books *We're Still Family* and *The Good Divorce*, have found that children of divorce can do well emotionally, socially, and academically. This positive outcome can happen when we do not involve kids in dissolutions. Along with the basic needs of food and shelter, what's most important for children are parents who can focus on the job of parenting and provide a stable home with love and discipline. According to Ahrons, parents do not need to live in the same home to raise well-adjusted kids; another important ingredient is a child does well when both parents maintain good relationships with the child.

Children should not have to suffer during a breakup. If a parent wants to tear his partner's life apart, this will affect the lives of the children. My family was conscious of this detail, and when my first marriage ended miserably, my kin was kind and accepting toward my ex-husband. However, I had no interest in compassion at the time. I was stuck in my daily negativity. Learning to be charitable and empathic was laughable; my mind kept hanging my ex by his toes. All of which felt satisfying, for a while. What changed my mind? There's a certain emptiness that lingers; plus I had witnessed numerous corrosive breakups of people who once loved each other, and the children were the end receivers.

Vitriol Isn't Worth the Pain

I learned to value having my ex-husband around after some time. He would come over for dinner, and I would keep a stiff upper lip for the sake of our sons. We even organized family vacations together. Because my mother was so adamant about proper titles, I thought we should give my ex-husband one, he had earned it. "What are we supposed to call him now?" I asked her.

"No word. Just 'Husband.'"

Baffled, I looked up the Hui term for former spouse and found *qianfu*. The concept of divorce was not allowed during my mother's time. The generations before us just didn't get decoupled, whether consciously or unconsciously. Therefore, my mother's nonchalant answer made sense. I realized my mom had entered new territory. She now had to maneuver a split union and children raised in separate homes. This may be why she was willing to keep my amiable ex-husband as kin.

My ex-husband is definitely a *much* more compassionate and bighearted person than I am, and I've learned that being accepting of others encourages health and well-being. I just wish someone told me that when I wanted to hang him by his toes.

Bringing more harmony into your life should be easy, but it

isn't always. In relationships where there is still conflict, sometimes it's better to be businesslike. This may sound cold and clinical, but treating an ex-partner like you would a work colleague is one strategy. You could start by making an offer to work together, providing a set of agreeable terms, being open to alternative options, and finding common ground. If one partner pushes back on something, the other partner listens and remains patient and respectful.

Getting along in relationships requires good emotion regulation, and being in touch with our feelings through physical awareness is a place to start: *What is my fidgeting telling me?* Deploying good regulation can reduce the intensity of our emotions, and it gives us time to react positively, rather than freaking or lashing out.

This can be hard when we deploy blame in our relationships; sometimes we blame others, and sometimes we blame ourselves. Blame generally sabotages our relationships. The thing to remember is that relationships take work. We can learn to shelve our pessimistic thoughts about our partners by coaxing each other's ideal selves into reality and bringing out the best in one another. We should regularly maintain our relationships by listening to each other with respect, trust, and honesty.

Relationships can work when we pay attention to the other person without judgment or a fixed agenda. This can help us understand where our partners are coming from. We can do so by paying attention to their body language, repeating what is being said, and being objective in order to see their point of view. Most important of all is being kind, grateful, and supportive.

Chapter Eight

Spirituality and Intuition Are Antidotes for Misery

There have always been Tibetan Buddhists in my family's homeland. The homeland is, after all, on the Tibetan–Qinghai Plateau. I once saw a monk traveling along a dirt road. He took a few steps forward, fell flat on his face, and got up. He repeated this exercise while chanting his holy mantra the entire path to the temple. There was something about seeing this that moved me.

When the Dalai Lama was a child, he traveled in a covered wagon to our hometown. My mother, also then just a child, poked her head out of her father's storefront and watched the commotion. The horses and mules were decorated in silk, and the carriages had embroidered canopies. Peeking from the front door, she saw the pint-size lama sitting inside an elaborate wagon.

Much later, I met the Dalai Lama in a blessing line. He pointed at me and asked, "Amdo?" Many Tibetans in Qinghai were and are from the Amdo region, and I look a little like them.

The prostrating monk and the famous lama made me curious

to learn more about where I came from. Seeing them also gave me a sense of wonder that encouraged hope and positivity. Witnessing something bigger than myself took me outside of myself. The Hui love the mysteries that surround existence; it makes day-to-day reality seem less mundane and more miraculous. My mother told stories that seemed *ooh* mystical and *ahh* otherworldly. She wanted to make life more exciting for the rest of us.

Spiritual Signs Are So Romantic

Many cultures believe in magical thinking, like money appearing in a cotton sack out of nowhere. This, of course, never happens, but if one is Hui, it's mandatory to believe that it could. And if the cotton sack appears in a surprising place like a grimy old outhouse, we're even luckier. Fortune, luck, and superstition are all part of magical thinking. It is spiritual to believe, and we feel good when we believe in something.

Of course, such thinking flies in the face of science. There's just no proof that things happen for a reason. Rationally speaking, seeing a sign of something magical means that we see something and not much else. Frankly, there is not much evidence or fact behind magical thinking. Logical me knows this. However, I admit that I embrace signs for the sake of mystery and intrigue regardless of what science has to say.

Even hardcore atheists connect patterns and knock on wood. Besides, and this is pure rationalization, acknowledging a sign may lead to being more open to new opportunities and positivity. Naturally, being open is a trait found in lucky and adaptable people. We might think that fortune finds the lucky person, but maybe an open mind simply leads to the possibility of fortune.

Many of us are altogether predisposed to spiritual mystery.

We hail phenomena from out of this world, and we like to think that "The Force" is real. Stories of the supernatural are enthralling. There are tales about people, often children, who recount things that happened in the past before they were even born. For instance, a boy named Christian Haupt told his mother when he was the age of two that he *was* a tall baseball player. He told her details about a ball player's life he could not have known—train trips, hotel stays, and even private grudges. These details matched up with events in Lou Gehrig's life.

Ian Stevenson of the University of Virginia School of Medicine looked into the previous life memories of children. He identified and studied thousands of cases around the globe, including places like Lebanon, India, Sri Lanka, and the US. At one point, Pulitzer Prize-winning journalist Tom Shroder followed Stevenson and documented many of these cases in his book *Old Souls: Compelling Evidence from Children Who Remember Past Lives.*

They found that children who claim memories of past lives are common. One boy had the memory of piloting a plane that was shot down by the Japanese during World War II. Another remembered that a group of men repeatedly stabbed him in the abdomen and threw him into a patch of blackberry bushes. One girl, before she knew how to speak in full sentences, kept trying to call her *husband* on the phone; she recalled the past life of a woman who had died after heart surgery. When the girl was older, family members of the woman who died came to visit the girl, and the girl asked them if they had received the jewelry she had bequeathed to them. She knew things no one knew.

In the end, Stevenson and Shroder had no conclusive determination about reincarnation; it may be possible, but they could not prove that it occurs.

There are also people with organ transplants who *feel* previous lives, namely the life of the person who donated their organ. Countless individuals have reported changes in their personality and predilections after their organ transplants. Post-operation, they suddenly have food cravings never experienced before—non-meat eaters have a hankering for a giant steak, or people who hate beer now love a good ale—and their taste in music or their level of risk-taking change.

Professional dancer Claire Sylvia, the author of the book *A Change of Heart: A Memoir*, wrote about post-surgery changes in her that were extraordinary—her life was recounted in the film *Heart of a Stranger*, starring Jane Seymour. She received a heart-lung transplant at Yale-New Haven Hospital from a young man named Tim who had died in a motorcycle accident; she took on his tastes and proclivities, including beer, green peppers, chicken nuggets, and curvaceous blondes. Her penchants came from nowhere.

Thomas Verny, a psychiatrist and author of *The Embodied Mind: Understanding the Mysteries of Cellular Memory, Consciousness, and Our Bodies*, has looked at this phenomenon. According to Verny, research suggests that a donor's organ can store memories. The memories may be encoded molecularly, which means that memory is perhaps beyond the brain.

Cellular memories or not, I want to believe in the mysticism of life and some kind of higher power. I might be thinking about my niece when suddenly she texts me, but is there any meaning to this? Probably not. However, I do want to think otherwise because it gives me hope that life is special—maybe, for me, things happen for a reason.

In his book, *The 7 Laws of Magical Thinking: How Irrational*

Beliefs Keep Us Happy, Healing, and Sane, science journalist and *New Yorker* writer Matthew Hutson cites research on why we believe in a higher power. Simply put, belief gives us a feeling of control. If everything happened randomly, we would not feel *any* control over our lives. The illusion of control may help us stand firmly on the ground. However, it is also possible that, when we think we're in control, we feel anxiety and negativity when things don't turn out the way we want. "People generally crave certainty and control. It's necessary for survival, so we look for it anywhere we might find it. Sometimes that leads us to see patterns in randomness and to project meaning onto the world. We become superstitious and religious," notes Hutson. Such magical thinking can help us handle the bumps in life, but it can also lead us astray. Perhaps we should just go with the flow.

Intuition Can Feel Spiritual

Going with the flow may also mean paying attention to the signals we get from within and from around us. Our instincts are real. Intuition is automatic and unconscious, and it's considered spiritual in many places in the world. In India, for example, gut instinct is considered a transcendent form of knowledge with a deep spiritual connection beyond our consciousness; intuitive experience is regarded as a state of enlightenment. We all have intuitions. Some people have spiritual conversations with their higher powers—at least my religious mother did. Regardless, there is something to this feeling that is also known as the *sixth sense*.

Putting aside our intuitive feelings can be a mistake. Someone I knew once told me she cried and cried on her wedding night. Her gut knew that there was something off; in time, her new husband started to gaslight her, and he made up much of their conflicts. "Why did you move my laptop?" he would accuse her even though she hadn't. She was blindsided by such accusations that came out of nowhere. In time, she learned that her husband was manipulative and wanted her to doubt herself. She had had a genuine feeling about her husband-to-be but didn't heed her instincts. When she finally filed for divorce, he opted for a *I'll-Make-You-Pay* split, and the end of their relationship was painful.

Some people call intuition magical thinking. Maybe it is. It is a feeling and can sometimes be faulty, mainly because people are generally biased; we have set beliefs and are looking for patterns. As a result, a person's intuition may be steered toward a belief or a pattern that feels morally and ethically wrong.

Most people have strong intuitions about morality, which are loaded with beliefs that are morally right to them. Some of my siblings, for example, had the instinct to share certain truths with our nonagenarian mother, who was often disturbed by the information they shared with her. Old people don't need to know if a couple within the family is experiencing conflict, or who is suffering a financial downturn. Sometimes I feel that you have to fib to protect people, especially old people. When ethical intuition is at work, our biases and beliefs can steer us incorrectly.

I dealt with Mom in her later years using a white-lie approach. I figured that there was no harm feigning complete ignorance over family affairs. My sister was less subtle and flat-out lied to her. At one point, she informed Mom that the car was irreparable. In all honesty, we wanted Mom to hang up the car keys and stop driving. I would argue that my sister's moral and ethical intuition in this case was quite accurate and helpful.

When we do pay attention to our intuition, we can at least weigh what we are dealing with. According to a 2019 research study appearing in the *Journal of Information and Knowledge Management Systems*, executives frequently use their intuition, which in turn, bolsters their confidence. They use this confidence in their decision-making by paying attention to what their bodies tell them. This may improve their intuitive awareness. Of course, they mine the data and analytics of their past experiences.

Executives use their intuition in their decision-making and with good results. Jeffrey David, entrepreneur and chairperson of the largest Nordic pet care company, has heeded his intuition again and again. He has found that deep stress turns off inner instinct, or at least it limits the capacity to source it. Stress brings on defensive decision-making and seems to diminish instinct. "When we are deep in battle, we can lose perspective and instinct," he said. "This happened during COVID. There was no benefit of time, time to pause and reflect." Instead, he and his team had to handle the healthcare of employees, to make sure they were safe. "Sometimes I lose the instinct, or at least I do not trust it." He felt that was a setback of sorts.

We are an amalgam of our life's experiences, and we access that data to fine-tune our navigation through life. To make an intuitive decision, David steps back and hovers over a situation like a detached and Buddhist moment. Otherwise, he thinks, we can overanalyze, and when we overanalyze, we do not tap into instinct. Hovering allows an unemotional decision or choice to emerge. It is subconscious, and he may not know why he is choosing one of three choices, yet he chooses through his gut instinct. To help this process, David often pulls himself out of a situation by driving his motorcycle or race car. During a ride, his brain is working in the background. "After a ride, I know what I need to do."

The unconscious mind puts feelings in our bones and looks through past experiences and the mind's collective expertise, as well as signs and cues from the world around us. In some ways, intuition relies much on expertise and knowledge. It is an unconscious intelligence, and like Jeffrey David, we cannot think too much about it.

Our Intuition Can Protect Us

Intuition may also be an alert for oncoming developments. The brain wants us to be alert to anything we should be aware of; that's when we may feel intuition upon us. Gut feelings warrant our attention. The mind is looking for things from the past that match the current experience. If a person we meet feels suspicious, we should tap into the sensation we are having.

Even the US military and law enforcement have been looking into our ability to hone our sixth sense to avoid risk and peril. A serviceman has to make decisions quickly. *Is that a roadside bomb? Does the person approaching me have hostile intent?* Former FBI agent Joe Navarro, author of *What Every Body Is Saying*, has been in many dangerous situations, but he listened to his intuition all the time. On certain occasions, he felt he should be cautious, and that his gut instinct was talking to him. *Don't enter that building. Wait for backup.* His intuition was usually right, especially when the location harbored a suspect with a gun.

Former petty officer first class Mark Almgren, who served in the Iraq War in 2010, was also trained to listen to his instincts. Every mission had to be well-planned. His job as rear gunner on convoys required that he hone his situational awareness into muscle memory. "I was trained to say something when the situation didn't feel right," he said. Otherwise, an ignored instinct may have resulted in a fatal outcome. He now trains military who are at high risk for capture—for example, air crew units including fighter pilots, technicians, and engineers who may get shot down. Almgren instructs those at potential high-risk to survive, evade, resist, and escape. "I train them to go with their gut," he says.

People may also have accurate premonitions about illness. Marin County-based Dustin Ballard has seen this in his work as a physician. People who are in tune with their bodies have hunches when they feel something is amiss with them physically. Migraines are a good example of this. People with migraines may have subtle warnings, known as prodrome symptoms, including feeling hypersensitive about lights and sounds or feeling anxious or irritable. Some pregnant women can also feel something amiss with their babies in utero. A 2011 survey that appeared in the journal *Acta Obstetricia et Gynecologica Scandinavica*, reported that some women who miscarried had a feeling about their pregnancy and that their baby was unwell.

Premonitions about illness also include foreboding feelings about death. A cousin of mine told me that her aunt said, "I am going to die tonight" and then died later that evening. Even pets can sense illness and death. A 2007 paper in *The New England Journal of Medicine* reported on a cat named Oscar that lived at the Steere House Nursing and Rehabilitation Center in Providence, Rhode Island. Oscar knew patients were dying and would curl up next to them, and they often died hours after he had cuddled up to them.

Spirituality Heals Us

We may feel better when we are in touch with our spirituality, and we can also benefit when we are connected with this part of ourselves. When we tap into our intuition and intangible experiences, we are more open. However, spirituality and religion are somewhat confusing. On the one hand, we are more likely to suffer if we are worried about hell, brimstone, and divine punishment. People who are more fearfully devout tend to suffer more mood disorders. On the other hand, people who openly embrace divine powers that are not punitive enjoy better well-being in general.

Neuroscientist Andrew Newberg, director of research with the Marcus Institute of Integrative Health at Jefferson University and author of *Neurotheology*, has examined the relationship between the mind and religion or spirituality through brain images of people practicing meditation and prayer. He found that these practices increase dopamine, the feel-good neurotransmitter associated with happiness.

He and other researchers have found that prayer and meditation are correlated with a higher sense of well-being. Generally, people who pray or meditate are less aggressive, kinder, forgiving, optimistic, compassionate, and often more flexible about life. In addition, when people pray together there's a feeling of unity, and being social benefits health and well-being. Those who call themselves spiritual are usually less stuck in unhappy mental loops.

Meditation works by being still and not thinking—or at least watching our thoughts float without distress or judgment. The body and mind can foster positive gene expression, the on-off switch that controls when and where molecules and proteins are made in the body. Positive gene expression from meditation can encourage lower levels of inflammation, which causes illness and disease, and a stronger immune system. Many research studies, including one published in a 2016 *Brain, Behavior, and Immunity* report, have found that meditation may decrease inflammation and increase antibodies and antiviral responses.

The much-cited work of the late Herbert Benson, founder of the Benson-Henry Institute for Mind Body Medicine and a professor at Harvard Medical School, examined the phenomenon of meditation. In his seminal book, *The Relaxation Response*, he described the mind's ability to relax the body—in brain activity, metabolism, breathing rate, and heart rate—which can happen through such a contemplative practice. He and colleagues studied monks in meditation as well and found that they can raise their body temperature by seventeen degrees and lower their metabolism by 64 percent. Having power and control over the mind and body would be a great achievement.

We Can All Be a Little Buddhist

I cannot change my body temperature whatsoever, and I don't want the dogma that devout religiosity can carry, but I do strive to be a little Buddhist. I would like to emulate their capacity for equanimity and compassion.

In its essence, Buddhism sees death and suffering as a fact of life. There is no negative view painted over suffering. It is part of existence. They see desire as a root of suffering; the longing for things, material or otherwise, keeps one in the morass of pain. Whether we believe in reincarnation or not, it is universal in all religions that doing good for other people can generate a positive flow that pulls us out of our heads. Benevolence pays forward, and good ethical behavior will see us through life's turns.

The basic tenets of Buddhism are codes of ethics we can live by to develop a higher character that may lead us on the path to enlightenment.

- Eliminate greed, hatred, and ignorance.
- Do not harm others.
- Put aside our egos and live with a clear mind.
- Recognize that our truth is ours, and our perspective is ours.
- Embrace ambiguity and uncertainty.
- Practice patience and more patience.
- Be generous—with our time, help, and possessions.
- Accept that life is suffering—suffering has a cause and an end.

How can we explain the things that just happen? How do children recall memories of past lives? How would they have the exact memories of people who have died? How do some people know when they are going to die?

Somehow we have a hunch and know things.

There isn't a lot of science behind magical thinking, but embracing the mystery of life can help us. Acknowledging a sign or omen may lead to openness, and this can lead to opportunities. We may be able to tap into the ethereal sides of ourselves, and prayer and meditation may help us do this. These practices are correlated with a higher sense of well-being. In addition, people who meditate or pray are less aggressive, kinder, and more optimistic. In this sense, spirituality may well help us out of our negative thinking patterns.

Chapter Nine

Be True and Genuine with Positivity

The celebrated psychologist Carl Rogers once said, "The curious paradox is that when I accept myself just as I am, then I can change." I will admit that I haven't always accepted myself as I am, especially after I got divorced. I was dating a person who was not entirely good for me. He badgered me about how to invest my money. People around me asked, "What are you doing with this guy? He's arrogant and insufferable."

"But when I was sick with pneumonia, he cared for me," I answered. I thought this argument would cancel out all his negative traits, but when he started to call a friend of mine, I asked him why. To this, he said, "If you have a problem with this, it's your problem. You're jealous and unreasonable." I am ashamed to say that I did not bolt right away.

We all want stability and safety, and it's natural to turn to others for care and protection. Yet looking inward is what we need to be doing. However, we can't do that when we suffer a disingenuous relationship with ourselves. Not being ourselves is problematic because we must live with ourselves all our lives. No one else can do it for us. When we're not on good terms with ourselves, we spend a lot of time looking over our shoulders. I used to do this. While looking over my shoulder, I also justified my choices, defended my actions, and rationalized my thinking. I was very much defensive inside my head back then.

I now know that I can depend on myself. I know what I value: my family and loved ones. My goal is to have harmony and warmth in my life. And all of this gives me the foundation to move forward.

When it comes to feeling solid and stable, we must first feel secure within ourselves. How do you feel when you think about yourself? Do you feel grounded and steady or unmoored and adrift? Even a grounded and secure individual must cope with and manage the stresses of life. Emotionally healthy people do not avoid the self. They don't look for ways to divert attention by streaming videos, shopping online, or thinking about what they will eat for their next meal. Instead, if they feel sad or angry or anxious, they may meditate—not ruminate—on why and how to feel more grounded.

The Importance of Personal Identity

American journalist and author John-Manuel Andriote had to learn how to be real with himself. He knew he was different, and from an early age, he hid the truth that he was not straight. He did this for many years. What bothered him the most was that he had to tell his mother. But when he did, his mother said to him, "Be brave."

Andriote took charge of his life and came out. He documented men who came of age during the AIDS epidemic in the 1980s. He chronicled their illnesses and deaths. He watched the man he loved fade and wither into nothing. Ultimately, he published the book titled *Victory Deferred: How AIDS Changed Gay Life in America*. This was his public way of being true to himself.

A solid identity and a strong sense of self can counter negativity and are essential for well-being. When we have relationships with people who have a strong sense of personal identity, there is more interdependence. A grounded individual does not railroad others with his beliefs, opinions, and feelings. This is called the "differentiation of self." Highly differentiated individuals hold onto their personal identities and can achieve healthy intimacy, connection, and a high level of respect in their relationships.

The late psychiatrist Murray Bowen, who created family systems therapy, formed the concept of differentiation of self. He viewed a family as an emotional unit, which comes with its own unique and complex interactions, as well as intense emotional connections. As the family matures, each member differentiates emotionally and physically from other members of the unit. A person who differentiates successfully can feel that she is her own person while maintaining a close attachment to others. A person with healthy differentiation does not look for acceptance, validation, or the approval of others. This person is neither a people-pleaser nor a chameleon who changes her self-projection to match others in her company. She can separate her feelings from thoughts and sustain how she feels and thinks even when under pressure from others. At the same time, she is not a bully who pushes others to adhere to her personal view. Obedience is not what she wants. A poorly differentiated person, conversely, may find herself in therapy for years. She may not dig deeply into her irrational and negative thoughts or behavior. She's just too busy tending to the turmoil of her day-to-day existence.

Such unsettled individuals can intermittently feel mental

confusion, low self-worth, insecurity, impulsivity, compulsivity, obsessiveness, hysteria, phobia, and other bleak and miserable mental states. A place for them to start course-correcting is learning who they are.

Deploying Bowen's concept of differentiation of self is an exercise in grounding one's identity. When we know who we are, we are surefooted and at peace with ourselves; we are able to quiet the negative noise inside our heads. A few things can help us get to this peace:

- Keeping a sense of individuality and not losing identity is paramount in relationships. This grounding feeds rational resolve rather than emotional reactivity.
- Differentiating the self heightens self-awareness. It helps us reflect productively on thoughts and feelings.
- A differentiated person is less likely to churn in their raw emotions.
- A differentiated person is able to set healthy boundaries and limits and remain individually autonomous while connecting emotionally with others.
- Distancing ourselves from intense, volatile people and situations can lead to better physical and mental health. Not removing ourselves can lead to burnout.

When we know who we are, a lot of nonsense, fear, cynicism, and mental discomfort fall away. We are less inclined to pose, brag, and put on fake airs. A grounded person knows what he is about.

Sooner or later, people embark on a soul-searching journey asking, "Who am I?" Yet in many cultures, asking this question is seen as a waste of time. According to Michael Puett and Christine Gross-Loh, who have authored books about philosophy from Chinese culture, people are messy and there doesn't seem to be one true self. Puett and Gross-Loh cite philosophies that show how people can be contradictory. We put on different personas in different settings. We may be more relaxed with family and close friends, on good behavior with the boss or customers, or more guarded with strangers.

We Worry About What Others Think

It's important to get along with other people, and it makes sense to manage relationships with care. Sometimes when we're interacting with others, however, we may bend ourselves a little too much—maybe so much that we do not recognize ourselves.

While there is likely no one *true self* per se, it helps when a person is honest and transparent, most especially with himself. This person doesn't engage in self-deception because lying to the mirror is useless. A solid person is hard to bully, does not blame others for his missteps, and is accountable for his decisions. He's not on a continual quest to reinvent himself. He is who he is.

When you know the people around you, there's no point in being condescending or boastful. In healthy non-dysfunctional relationships, there's no point in seeking approval to feel valued. You should already feel this way from those around you. Plus, because of the safety of your tribe, perceptions of reality are solid. Everyone knows your name, so to speak. In effect, it is safe to be *you*.

A person who is not genuine with himself is dishonest with himself. For Brené Brown, a professor at the University of Houston and author of *Daring Greatly: How the Courage to Be Vulnerable Transforms the Way We Live, Love, Parent, and Lead* (among many other books), a person who thinks she has an idea of who she *is supposed to be* may be far from who she *truly is*. Being untrue to oneself is a foundation for true unhappiness and mental discord.

When you know who you are and what you value, you will be okay with life's ups and downs. If we adhere to the thinking of University of Nevada psychologist Steven Hayes, this is important. Knowing who you are at the core and what is important to you will remove what hinders you from living a meaningful life. Knowing with clarity what a meaningful life looks like *for you* is at the heart of your mental harmony and true contentment. For example, does climate change bother you? Then get outside and volunteer with an environmental group. Focus on what matters and leave the rest behind.

According to Stephen Joseph, a professor of psychology at the University of Nottingham and author of the book *Authentic: How to Be Yourself and Why It Matters*, an authentic person who is true to herself is emotionally mature and speaks the truth, even when the truth hurts. Sincere people:

- Know their reality and what they want in life. Knowing what they value is key.
- Are introspective and understand themselves.
- Are kind and compassionate toward themselves and others.
- Own up to their mistakes and learn from them.
- Welcome and express their emotions.

The Cultivation of Compassion

I once worked with a person who fretted about a lot of things. She would ask me questions like "Do I annoy you?" Or, "Do you think

I did a good job on that project?" Wherever she is now, I hope she has applied some self-compassion and is living a richer life. Applying self-compassion can help a person find her authentic self.

Imagine flipping a switch and speaking to yourself with less emotional intensity. This could mean speaking to yourself as if you were discussing a business plan with someone in a more objective manner, especially when there's potential for anxiety, anger, or any number of heated emotions. Speaking to the self with compassion can mean improved overall well-being. Author Toni Bernhard has lived for decades with chronic pain, and she shares firsthand knowledge about it in her books, including *How to Be Sick*. The foremost item on her list of topics is the benefit of being kind to oneself. The former University of California at Davis law professor said, "Attacking the self can come too readily. We often feel we aren't even worthy of kindness toward ourselves."

Indeed, we tend to be hard on ourselves. When bad things happen—the death of a loved one, for example—some of us are quick to flog ourselves with judgmental self-loathing. "I should have said I loved her more often. I deserve all my pain and suffering. I am such a loser." Internalizing a negative self-view pushes us down both mentally and physically. We may suffer more depressive thoughts, anxiety, neuroticism, and lower self-worth. These mental health concerns increase the risk of stress, and in turn compromise well-being in the forms of lower immunity, poorer cardiovascular health, risk of infections, and other physical problems. The mind affects the body, of course.

How can we instill more open thinking, kindness, and positivity, and fight the inclination toward internal misery as well? One answer is by talking to ourselves in a more hopeful and beneficial way. Self-talk can be decidedly damaging. Think of the phrase:

"Why am I such an idiot?" We didn't speak to ourselves like this when we were small. Little children are wide-eyed with wonder, imagination, and excitement. "The flower smells like an apple. Can I bite it?" They are also their own cheering squads. "I can hop to the tree on one leg. Watch me." Unfortunately, this exuberance can get squashed by an authoritarian parent or a crabby teacher.

The child then acquires a negative inner voice filled with dread, anxiety, anger, and self-defeat. Nothing is good. Everything is bad. The child learns to nurse his fault-finding and vehemently devalues himself. With the brain's negative default, such self-flagellation can be relentless. It doesn't always come in the form of self-talk either. We sometimes visualize the gloominess, or we can feel it physically. I know I have done this when I bypass the inner verbal dialogue and feel dreadful in my body.

A child can develop a running interior narrative that says there has to be something wrong with him and that he deserves his parent's ire and unending criticism. Such a strategy isn't a good way to motivate a young person as negative feedback leads to private brow-beating. For example, we don't have control over events that just happen, yet we may be quick to take the blame. "I should have checked the brakes before she drove off. It was all my fault that the car skidded into the tree." But an accident is just an accident.

When You Are Not Kind to Yourself

Internal animus can pave the way to self-destructive habits, like poor emotion regulation in the form of anxiety or even addictive behaviors or self-harm. The silent monologue within a person who drowns herself in self-criticism can be littered with blame. Yet would that person treat a friend in the same way? "You're incompetent and unworthy. Go ahead, sink yourself in your bad habits. Who cares?" Who would say these words to someone else? Mark White, a professor of philosophy at the City University of New York and author of books such as *The Decline of the Individual*, has written extensively on the topic of self-loathing. He has pointed out that it's hard to love a self-loathing person, one who will monitor every word you utter and worry that he has said or done something wrong. The self-loathing person will look to you to fill in the missing pieces in himself and may reject your help, thinking he's not worthy, noted White.

However, a person can flip his inner dialogue toward the positive. This is good for building empathy, considering other viewpoints, tolerating distress, reaching goals, and regulating emotions. Moreover, positive self-talk can promote well-being. When you boost yourself, you can experience higher self-worth and improved overall physical health.

When you are aware of your internal angst, it can give way to self-kindness. When compassion starts with you, it comes back to you. Compassion can then flow freely in your social network. We know it's difficult to help a person who is not kind to herself, which also means it's hard to accept help from a person who is not kind to herself. Members of a family, a community, a nation, or even the world, for that matter, are all symbiotic agents in an interconnected system. The flow of compassion wants to move freely.

Defeat Negative Self-Talk

We all feel miserable at times. It's normal. It's okay to feel 100 percent rotten. Compassion for yourself during these moments will lend you clarity, self-respect, and meaning. However, being kind to yourself may be one of the hardest challenges. Here are a few things to think about:

- To be kind to others, we have to start with ourselves and be our own best friends.
- Treat the self like we would treat a friend.
- Look at our thoughts and feelings without judgment or criticism.
- Let ourselves make mistakes. Mistakes open the door to self-growth.

We have learned that we can depend on ourselves. But we must first feel secure within ourselves. The emotionally healthy person does not avoid himself; he has a solid identity and a strong sense of self. This can fight the baked-in negativity we all suffer. Psychologists like Brené Brown, Carl Rogers, and Murray Bowen know that a grounded person does not look for acceptance, validation, or the approval of others. If we do, we are unsettled, and we can feel mental confusion, low self-worth, insecurity, impulsivity, compulsivity, and other miserable states.

A grounded person knows what he is about, he knows who he is, is surefooted, and at peace with himself. A solid person also gets along with other people. However, we should probably not bend ourselves so much that we cannot recognize who we are.

A person who is not genuine with himself is likely to be dishonest with himself. If we know who we are and what we value, we will be okay. That is why we need to know what a meaningful life looks like for us. That is our beacon. And if we can instill more open thinking, kindness, and positivity, we can fight the inclination toward internal misery.

Chapter Ten

We Need Validation

At certain moments in life, we do not feel so wonderful, and we look for some acknowledgment of this. Whenever my mother asked me how I was in those moments, the best answer I could give without feeling dishonest was "okay," to which she would say, "Live through my life and you should feel more than just okay." Eventually, I learned not to go to her when I needed validation for my feelings. I went to my sister instead because she was so much better at making me feel heard, and I also eventually learned how to validate myself.

More recently, my son said to me, "Mom, when I'm telling you about my crummy day, just say, 'That sucks.'" There I was giving him ideas on how to solve his problems; in truth, I was invalidating him. I know I have to actively work toward validating the feelings of others, *especially* my kids. Whatever age a child may be, they need a parent's validation.

Certainly, some people regularly cry and moan with

sky-is-falling misery, and they do so over the smallest things. This is the histrionic personality type who loves to wade and bask in the agony and distress of the everyday. It's an exaggerated melodrama that perhaps makes them feel alive, and maybe it's something they learned from their family of origin. All the attention is on the aggrieved person, and she must keep the attention on herself at every moment. But the rest of us may think, *Please don't bask in each catastrophe like you're the star of everyone else's soap opera*. This may be related to what psychiatrist Stephen Karpman called the Drama Triangle, in which people get stuck in a victim-rescuer-persecutor dynamic. Karpman wrote about this in his book *A Game Free Life*, an analysis of dysfunctional relationships.

Seeking Validation in the Age of Social Media

When I was younger, I wished my parents celebrated birthdays. I dreamed of big chocolate cakes, candles, ice cream, and a mountain of presents, but my parents never fussed over any milestone. I was seven years old when I attended a birthday party, my first ever. I couldn't understand what was going on. Why were adults celebrating this child? I don't think I ever received any presents. I only remember wrapping them for other people's children. Gift-giving within my family was just not done. None of us sang songs chiming, "I am special." My mother impressed upon us the value of humility. Later, my sister told me, "They didn't want us to become spoiled." That sounds good in theory, but maybe they went a little too far.

I guess my parents were ahead of Jean Twenge's time. Twenge is a professor of psychology at San Diego State University who has examined entitlement in young people. Her books include *Generation Me: Why Today's Young Americans Are More Confident, Assertive, Entitled—and More Miserable Than Ever Before*, as well as *The Narcissism Epidemic: Living in the Age of Entitlement*. She has argued that American culture is focused on money, fame, and appearance, all markers of self-involvement. Just think of the way reality TV came and never went away.

Social media's pings, tweets, and clicks feed the need to display the self in self-absorbed selfies. *Look at me, world. I'm having more fun than anyone else, even you.* The Internet goads a person into pumping himself up. Nowadays, we can announce ourselves online with videos and images of our gripping lives. The narrative is "It's all about me." This chronicle is a highly curated account that shows high-drama bad days where the world is against the protagonist. Some people play this lead figure with so much spectacle that it can turn fictional and sometimes even delusional. While there is no official term or diagnosis for "main character syndrome," the phenomenon has been bandied about in popular culture for a while.

When you're the main character, everything that happens happens to you. Are you sitting in a traffic jam because of the blizzard? Of course, it's all about you. Your friends didn't text you back immediately? How dare they. The main character needs an audience to witness how life is so hard, so amazing, so shocking, and so sensational. This does not mean that the person is necessarily a narcissist, but it can become problematic when it goes from self-absorption to self-delusion. Self-delusion can lead to insecurity and a desperate mindset. Social media fuels the round-the-clock tendency to nurture this self-delusion.

According to Lawrence White, a professor of psychology

at Beloit College and the author of *Culture Conscious: Briefings on Culture, Cognition, and Behavior*, various factors have influenced the growing focus on the self across the world, namely affluence, urbanization, plenty of technology, and online connection. These features of society have pushed individualism and the feeling of "I am important" across the globe. In a *Journal of Cross-Cultural Psychology* report, the usage of the words *we* and *our* has decreased, while the usage of *me* and *mine* has increased.

This me-centered mindset encourages the circulation of negative thoughts and a closed perspective. It can stoke envy, jealousy, and inflexibility. In a study published in the journal *Personality and Individual Differences*, being self-centered can lead to loneliness and poor well-being, and it can also mean suboptimal coping and rumination. By and large, the mindset of self-absorption is connected to negative dark traits.

The Dark Triad

The Dark Triad is a concept and personality cluster that was established by researchers Delroy Paulhus and Kevin Williams from the University of British Columbia, and it highlights the traits of narcissism, Machiavellian behavior, and psychopathy or sociopathy. Narcissists are grandiose, ego-driven, and devoid of empathy. The Machiavellian is the manipulator who is happy to deceive and exploit others for personal gain. Meanwhile, psychopaths and sociopaths, some of whom are capable of fatal harm and feel no remorse whatsoever, are selfish and callous with no regard for others.

The dark traits of narcissism and manipulation are significantly correlated with negative emotions. Generally, people with dark tendencies are not content. They are negative and more prone to bleak thinking than other people. Their need to be in the spotlight of attention—a necessity for approval—and their unhappiness and insecurities are at the root of this negativity. This negativity can spread to others.

While there is a genetic component to narcissism, it doesn't mean the trait is fixed. Narcissistic qualities surface in most school-aged children. We felt "it's all about me" at very young ages. However, parents can help encourage or discourage these characteristics.

Sometimes we pump up children to make them feel extraordinary: "Wow, you hit the ball. You are so amazing." This encouragement of surface-level uniqueness can sometimes backfire. A child may walk away with an overblown sense of self, feeling that he deserves excess admiration. Parents sometimes make the mistake of showering the wrong type of praise. For instance, a child who studies hard should be praised for studying hard, not because he was born smart.

When children have an overblown sense of self, they grow into adults who think they are superior to others and tend to forgo cooperation and teamwork. They prefer competition and dislike losing. Narcissists do not know how to improve themselves, get along, or feel compassion. They hold onto their individualism, believing that nothing else matters.

There's no question that individualism thrives in American culture. The Western workplace encourages us to be distinct: "There is no one like me. I am indispensable." And we value self-expression: "I gotta be me." There is also the notion that one needs a good dose of narcissism to be successful. We avoid conformity and embrace singularity. Being quirky and different is the way to *win*.

Yet with the aim toward extreme uniqueness, finding common ground can be difficult. Someone who prides herself on her extraordinary X-factor qualities might have a tough time stepping into another person's shoes and therefore would be hard-pressed to feel another's pain. Societies that promote such individualism score lower on the empathy scale than those promoting community.

Me, Me, Me

Then there are the *very* dark sides of individualism. Malevolent traits may flourish in "me, me, me" conditions. Malignant narcissists harbor grandiosity, entitlement, and callousness, as well as a need for external approval and admiration. They are essentially needy, thoroughly unhappy, and negative.

Brené Brown thinks that some people suffer the shamed-based fear of being ordinary. This distress is rampant in many industries, but show business is perhaps the most spotlighted. It's a field of work where people can *grow* into their misery and negativity. A former agent at a talent management firm met with many demanding actors who swaggered into her office needing adoration. One was handsome and talented, yet he was B- or C-list at best. He said with conviction, "I am talented. I went to Juilliard. I look like this. Why didn't I get that role? Why am I not more famous?" The agent surmised that this handsome low-list actor was extremely hard to work with on set. *Who would hire him?* she mused.

Validation Should Not Be About People-Pleasing

People who cannot live without validation may seek approval

and be people-pleasers. However, trying to please others and looking for approval doesn't work because it's impossible to please everyone. It also creates the fear of rejection. Intrinsically, people-pleasing has to do with low self-esteem and a fear of being dismissed; people-pleasers often have difficulty setting boundaries, resent others for not appreciating them, want to be perfect, and compromise what they value.

Certainly, we want to stay within the good graces of our tribe. If we are banished, we must fend off other tribes and dangers in the unknown and unfriendly wild. Exclusion does sting. But the idea of being banished just because we don't agree with the next person sounds severe. I would be better off without such scrutiny.

Every person wants to be seen and heard. Validation is important for emotional health. Otherwise, we feel denied and judged. However, what matters most is the validation of the *self.* We have to matter to *ourselves* first:

- Disapproval from others does not have to be our problem or reality.
- Recognition from others is needed at a young age, but we can also recognize ourselves later in life.
- Our approval of ourselves is most important, and the inner experience is real.
- Recognizing our feelings is fundamental to internal validation.
- Accepting ourselves is part of self-compassion, and doing this will help remedy the internal distress we feel.

Counting our blessings and not looking for external validation can help us. For a few minutes after my yoga session each morning,

I lay on my back and think about the little things that make me smile. Mostly, how my husband makes me toast in the morning, my son calls to check on me, my ex says hello, and my niece texts me to ask after my day. These tiny interactions have a big impact. I can't help but feel loved and lifted. I realize that this informal cataloging of "smile memories" is my idea of a gratitude list.

These smile memories, however, do not exactly make up a proper gratitude inventory, as researched by Robert Emmons, a social psychologist at the University of California at Davis and the author of many books including *Gratitude Works!: A 21-Day Program for Creating Emotional Prosperity*. His studies measured well-being through writing down feelings of gratitude. People who do this are more optimistic, have fewer physical ailments, and spend more time on self-care.

According to various cross-cultural researchers, Americans could use some reminders to be grateful. However, in other places around the world, feeling gratitude is already part of one's internal makeup. In more communal cultures, people think about doing better for their group rather than for themselves. South Koreans, for example, feel a decline in well-being after writing thank-you letters because they reflect on their inadequate contributions to their group or community. Instead of doing these gratitude exercises, communally oriented people would rather do good for their tribe.

Give with the Heart

A good way to boost internal validation is through helping others. When we are altruistic, feel-good hormones like dopamine increase. Essentially, we feel good about ourselves when we help others.

During my mom's youth, when the poor called at the front

gate, family members took turns handing out food and money. Family members did not ignore the needy. Giving had to be done and done with respect. The number of homeless people who visited the family's front gate increased on any given holiday. They were tired and careworn, but they carried their bowls and looked genuinely grateful for any morsel shared. They were not shunned and cast aside like vermin.

In places like New York City, I regularly see people holding signs that read, *I am short $29.65 for the bus ride home to Grand Rapids. Please help me get home.* People walk by the homeless like they don't exist. Often, I see the same people holding the same signs on different street corners. We have become numb and helpless when we see destitute people.

Research published in *The Journal of Social Psychology* examined study subjects who engaged in a variety of kind acts toward people they were close to, as well as people they weren't close to. After seven days of engaging in these various acts or just by observing, the subjects enjoyed increased happiness. Being kind helps the world in a positive way, and it also helps maintain the positivity within *ourselves.*

Sara Konrath, at the University of Michigan, has examined the topic of altruism for years. She and her colleagues wondered how empathy works around the world. They found that certain regions are more group-oriented. Therefore people from these places score higher on empathy scales and are more apt to be super-empathizers as well. A group-oriented person sees himself as just one individual among many others. This person perceives harmony in one's group and community as most important.

Of course, among North Americans, giving can take on different meanings. In one study published in the *Nonprofit and Voluntary Sector Quarterly*, researchers surveyed 819 subjects in the US. Their reasons for giving included tax breaks, appearing decent in the eyes of others, or donating to a certain charity when it mattered to a loved one. And, of course, another good reason is a simple concern for other people.

Spread the Kindness and Gratitude

Kindness and gratitude have an evolutionary foundation. They are basic necessities for survival. We give gratitude for the help we get from others, and we get gratitude for the help we give to others. Kindness and gratitude make us happier, less depressed, and more positive about life. We are more likely to engage in self-care. Feeling kind and grateful can even affect how we eat as we tend to make healthier food choices when we are feeling kind and grateful.

A 2018 study that appeared in the journal *Psychotherapy Research* monitored 300 people, mostly college students, who sought and received counseling for their depression and anxiety. These participants were divided into three random groups—one group received only counseling, one group was asked to write down how they felt about their negative experiences, and one group was asked to write a gratitude letter to three different people, one letter a week over three weeks. Among the three groups, the people who wrote grateful letters experienced better mental health four weeks and twelve weeks after sending the letters.

These expressions of appreciation can come in different forms, and they can describe what the person did, and how it affected us. We don't even have to write letters. We can spend time in the company of loved ones and tell them how much they mean to us. It also does not have to involve a person. The acknowledgment can be shared with a pet, or with nature when sitting under a tree—thanking the sky works.

We Can Be Less Interested in Ourselves

Thomas Gilovich is a social psychologist at Cornell University, as well as the author of many books, including *How We Know What Isn't So: The Fallibility of Human Reason in Everyday Life*. He and his colleagues have reported in the *Journal of Personality and Social Psychology* that people are too busy being interested in themselves, and that this may be why they don't always register the presence of others.

He and his colleagues also found that we have the perception that everyone else is having way more fun than we are. The average person may compare himself with the most socially adept individual in the room. This comparison makes him feel below average, with fewer friends and fewer invitations—just an average Joe living a mediocre existence. However, not everyone can be below the real average. Being generally interested in themselves, people worry about how we view them; they are not worried about us. All of us could try focusing on other people and less on ourselves; doing this may mean more giving and less taking, among everyone. It also means more positivity and less negativity for everyone.

Go Toward the Light Triad

The personality cluster of the Light Triad was developed by researchers from the Positive Psychology Center at the University of Pennsylvania including Scott Barry Kaufman, the author of *Transcend: The New Science of Self-Actualization*. They formed a three-legged counterpoint to the dark traits. This view can help us be more accepting of other people, be more open to new experiences, and even be more conscientious—all good traits if you want to get along with others positively.

According to a report in the journal *Frontiers in Psychology*, the light triad means having a loving and benevolent orientation toward others. The three legs of the light triad are:

Faith in Humanity: Believing that people are fundamentally good-willed.

Humanism: Believing that all people should be bestowed with dignity and respect.

Kantianism: Believing that people should not be used as puppets and pawns for any one person's gain.

Traits of this lightness include:

- Feeling secure in relationships.
- Tolerance of other perspectives.
- No need for power over others.
- Feeling humility and openness.
- Highly agreeable.
- High life satisfaction.
- High intellectual curiosity.

New York Times columnist David Brooks, the author of the book *The Road to Character*, has argued that modesty and humility are much more valuable than overconfidence and sky-high self-esteem. Humility as a foundation is more likely found in other cultures like Asia and Africa. It's a bedrock of many, if not all, philosophies around the world, and it leads to empathy and the ability to see life from another person's perspective. Humility and empathy guide us to look outward and not inward. This is useful when living a life of character and hopefulness.

Many theories try to explain human behavior by categorizing personality types—the Big Five or 16-factor, for example. I, for one, am conscientious and often more agreeable than

I should be. Being too conscientious can bleed into being too agreeable and can make a person easily manipulated. People who are too agreeable should be mindful of being too generous with money or getting passed over for a deserved promotion. I know I have these tendencies and have learned to change my behavior.

One theory, Raymond Cattell's 16-factor personality model, addresses the traits of temperament, motivation, emotion, creativity, achievement, and others. According to Cattell, humans are driven by basic motivations like hunger, curiosity, anger, and fear.

The Big Five is a template of personality that many researchers prefer. It has helped people understand personality differences and why they react to the world in the way they do. The Big Five has endured in the lexicon. It includes openness, conscientiousness, extraversion, agreeableness, and neuroticism. A further theory, the H-Factor or HEXACO adds the traits of honesty and humility. University of Calgary psychologist Kibeom Lee and Brock University psychologist Michael Ashton developed this model of personality that includes humility, emotionality or neuroticism, extraversion, agreeableness, conscientiousness, and openness to experience. The H-Factor or HEXACO is gaining ground and spotlights character. It addresses, for example, the inclination to obey the law or commit a crime—a person low in honesty and humility would be more likely to be deceptive, grandiose, sly, and conspicuous, among other characteristics.

How does a person see power, money, and sex, and does that person put others over himself? Mother Teresa, for example, was probably high in H-Factor—honesty and humility—and was not likely motivated by power or sex.

Understanding personality traits can help us develop more

humility, and doing so may help us counter the tendency to be self-focused and me-centered.

Nurture Intellectual Humility

Duke University social psychologist Mark Leary, the author of *The Curse of the Self: Self-Awareness, Egotism, and the Quality of Human Life*, has noted that intellectual humility is the opposite of intellectual arrogance, in which a person feels that his perspective is the right and only perspective. A person high in intellectual humility:

- Is not hell-bent on being right all the time.
- Understands that his thinking may be fallible.
- Is not stuck on his own awesomeness.
- Welcomes different outlooks and perspectives.

People are normally very busy being interested in themselves. They worry about how they are viewed and don't always worry about others. We can move toward the Light Triad by having a kind and benevolent orientation toward others. This humility and empathy can guide us to look outward and not inward.

What matters most is the validation of the *self.* We have to matter to *ourselves.* We can do this by writing down our feelings of gratitude, which can bring more optimism and fewer physical ailments. We can also do this by helping others as altruism boosts internal validation. We feel good about ourselves when we help others. Being kind and grateful makes us happier, less depressed, and more positive.

Chapter Eleven

The Body Knows What It Needs

My grandma used to wedge a stick of rosewood incense under a smooth flat rock that sat on a table in the corner of her bedroom. She tied a short length of thread through the square hole of a round coin, which would hang over the incense. When the incense burned down to the thread, the coin would then fall into a metal pan right below, the sound of which was supposed to wake her. Yet she was always up two minutes before the coin dropped into the pan.

For many people, the value of treating the body right has been handed down through the ages. The generations before us knew not to mess around with our bodies. Every day, our grandparents went to bed and woke at the same time. And most importantly, they didn't get upset over a fitful night of sleep. I think that relying on an alarm clock, as my grandma ultimately didn't, is a good sign that you're *not* in tune with your body's rhythms. Our physical well-being affects our mental state—it can flip negative to positive and vice versa.

When your body feels off-kilter, you know something is wrong, and this can negatively affect your mood. A good night's sleep is essential for a balanced, happy life. Yet people are plagued with insomnia and other sleep difficulties. According to the National Sleep Foundation in 2021, about 45 percent of Americans reported that insufficient sleep affected their waking activities at least once a week. The National Center for Health Statistics estimates that one in six adults have a diagnosed sleep disorder and one in eight adults who suffer these troubles use sleep aids.

For many people, the mind is not a friend to healthy sleep habits. Racing thoughts and the gravitational pull of pessimism often appear in those who suffer from anxiety, stress, depression, the side effects of medication, and other problems and conditions. Naturally, when there is nothing to do but lay in bed, the mind races in the dead of night.

Eric Haseltine is a neuroscientist formerly with the National Security Agency and the author of *Long Fuse, Big Bang: Achieving Long-Term Success through Daily Victories.* His entire working life has been rooted in psychology and neuroscience. You might think that such a researcher wouldn't have insomnia. Yet like many of us, he was the victim of having anxiety about the anxiety of not falling asleep. The brain's terrible tendency to buzz when the head hits the pillow vexes many people.

Haseltine's father also had a problem with insomnia. A rocket scientist at the Naval Air Weapons Station China Lake in California, his father was a polymath of sorts and had an intense interest in visual perception. He had learned about phosphenes, the specks and squiggles of light we see when we close our eyes. Phosphenes are caused by stimulation of the retina or activity in the neurons of the brain's visual system. His father started to focus on these specks when he went to bed. However, he often fell asleep before making any useful observations about them.

When this rocket-scientist father shared this tip with his neuroscientist son, the son tried the trick himself, and with great success, he fell asleep. Eric even experienced hypnagogic visions, which are images of patterns, shapes, or people we sometimes see when we are about to fall asleep. Ultimately, this could possibly be one way of dealing with insomnia.

Be Good to Your Body at Least for Your Mind's Sake

We must treat our bodies with love and kindness. Your body is your best friend, one that will keep your mind intact. Embracing healthy habits and being kind to the body may lead to a longer, healthier, happier, and more positive life. To start, there is essential self-care to engage in.

Eat a healthy diet of fruits, vegetables, complex carbs, and lean protein. Healthy eating means at least half your plate should be filled with colorful fruits and veggies like beets, red cabbage, tomatoes, squash, carrots, strawberries, blueberries, and more. A diet of plant-based foods increases and stabilizes the good bacteria in your gut microbiome—the ecosystem of microbes that live in your intestines and can keep you healthy.

This ecosystem also requires complex carbs. Whole grains like oats and brown rice are better than white bread, white rice, and refined grains. They are high in fiber, slow digestion and glucose absorption, and do not disturb blood glucose levels. This results in a gradual and steady rise in blood sugar, which reduces stress on the body.

We also need protein, the body's building blocks. Protein

is present in our muscles, bones, skin, and hair. Protein builds and repairs these and other tissues. It is also good for hormones and enzymes that regulate the immune system, among other functions. Fish, poultry, beans, and nuts are recommended, but limit your red meat intake.

Avoid processed foods and transfats like margarine, shortening, and fried foods. Instead, use non-hydrogenated oils such as canola, safflower, or olive. Also, avoid processed foods like crackers, chips, breakfast cereals, sodas, and packaged goods like cookies, among other items. Processed foods have little nutritional value, and contain unhealthy fats, sugar, sodium, preservatives, and artificial ingredients.

The gut speaks to the brain and, like the brain, it produces neurotransmitters, including dopamine and serotonin that regulate mood and anxiety. Fundamentally, a happy gut helps support a happy outlook.

In addition to healthy eating, there are other ways to be good to your body for your mind's sake:

Maintain a proper body mass index (BMI). To calculate your BMI, divide your weight in pounds by your height in inches squared. A high BMI indicates high body fat and a low BMI indicates low body fat. A healthy BMI is between 18.5 and 24.9. The BMI is used to estimate whether a person is overweight or underweight. It can help identify problems like type-2 diabetes, heart disease, high blood pressure, malnutrition, or anemia.

Limit your alcohol intake. A 2023 research paper in The Lancet Rheumatology reports that no amount of alcohol consumption is considered safe. Alcohol can increase the risk of many problems, including heart disease, liver damage, certain cancers, stroke, memory, and dementia, among others.

Practice good sleep hygiene. This means keeping a consistent schedule of seven to eight hours a night by rising at the same time and going to bed at the same time every night. It also helps to avoid electronics an hour before bed, limit daytime napping, and avoid large meals, caffeine, and alcohol four hours before bed. Plus the bed should be for sleeping rather than other activities like watching television or paying bills.

Of course, do not smoke. This may seem like a no-brainer, but smoking accelerates aging to a great degree, according to a report from a 2020 study in *Scientific Reports*. It can age a person by two decades. The study of about 500,000 people showed that smoking damages telomeres, whereby the ends of chromosomes get shortened in the white blood cells of the immune system. Short telomeres mean we age.

Engaging in self-care can alter a person's mental outlook. It can boost mood, lower stress, raise self-worth, and encourage a better perspective in life. In a study published in the journal of *International Journal of Nursing Studies*, researchers reasserted that self-care leads to better well-being and lower morbidity and mortality. A study published in the journal *Circulation* reported that middle-aged men who abided by the simple rules of self-care lived twelve years longer than men who completely eschewed them. Women benefitted even more, living fourteen years longer.

The Vagus Nerve for the Mind and Body

If we want to care for our minds and bodies, we should be aware of the mind-body superhighway, the vagus nerve. In Latin, *vagus* means wandering. This wandering nerve is the longest cranial nerve, and it passes through and links parts of the body, starting at the base of the brain, down the neck, through the chest, heart, lungs, abdomen, and intestines. It is part of the autonomic nervous system that controls the internal organs, and it is a pathway of the parasympathetic nervous system.

Stephen Porges, professor of psychiatry at the University of North Carolina at Chapel Hill and author of *The Polyvagal Theory*, has studied the vagus nerve and found that the autonomic nervous system and its vagus nerve regulate our health and behavior. This nerve is instrumental in the body's responses. It is why we sneeze, sweat, cough, and vomit, among other reflexes. It regulates the body's organ functions including heart rate, breathing, blood pressure, and digestion.

The vagus nerve alerts us to danger, helping the body move from flight and fight to its relaxation response. It helps us fight anxiety, increases blood flow, and can reduce inflammation. When your heart pumps in excitement and your stomach twitches with butterflies, the vagus nerve is at work. When we feel stress, cognition and executive function shut down, cutting off social connections and promoting negativity.

The body is happiest when this nerve is functioning and in balance; the vagus nerve wants to keep us safe and can calm and regulate the mind and body. It is also important in keeping us in good health through fighting disease. It can reduce the stress hormone cortisol in depression and anxiety patients, reduce pro-inflammatory cytokines in diseases like Crohn's and rheumatoid arthritis, reduce high blood pressure, and promote healthy gut function and alleviate irritable bowel syndrome. In addition, stress and anxiety can harm the gut's lining, which can allow toxins to enter the bloodstream. The vagus nerve helps us fight this.

There are ways to activate the vagus nerve:

- Splash cold water on your face. Cold water can activate this nerve by slowing the heart rate and redirecting blood flow to the brain.
- Sing, hum, laugh. This nerve is connected to the vocal cords. The larynx and pharynx in the throat are affected by the vibration, and this stimulates your vagus nerve.
- Meditate. Conscious breathing can increase vagal tone.
- Movement. Yoga, qigong, and tai chi postures can stimulate this nerve.

When the body feels unease, the mind dives into distress and negativity. If we stimulate the vagus nerve, we can combat this discomfort. The simple act of measured breathing can help the vagus nerve pull us back to calm. The opposite of this is holding one's breath, which puts us into the flight-fight-freeze response. This is when fear and anxiety take hold. Deep breathing is a physiological tool that can help keep negative thoughts in check. Breathing from the diaphragm, where the chest and the abdomen meet, is a technique that essentially flips a switch in the autonomic nervous system. When the sympathetic nervous system is triggered, the body tenses up, the heart rate increases and the blood vessels contract. Conversely, when we take a deep breath, the parasympathetic nervous system sets in and reduces stress, inflammation, and bodily tension.

How to Take a Deep Breath

Some of us need medication to manage our stress, anxiety, and depression, but the addition of meditation and breathwork can be very effective. A thoughtful exhale is a big part of mindfulness, and mindfulness is the opposite of mindlessness. I'd rather be mindful than mindless. The 4-7-8 yogic breathing practice works for me, especially when I'm trying to fall asleep. This is one way to do it:

- Breathe out.
- Close the mouth and take a deep breath in four counts through the nose.
- Hold the breath for seven counts.
- Open the mouth and exhale through the mouth in eight counts.
- Repeat until relaxed.

Why You Need to Move Your Body

Moving around is good for you from head to toe. I have seen firsthand what happens when we do or don't follow this directive. My sister was the kind of person who would rather sit and talk over many cups of tea. When she was in her fifties, I gave her a pedometer. However, the device found its way to the back of her junk drawer. This tendency of hers worried me. Once, while visiting a friend, she stumbled and broke a bone close to her hip. This led to surgery, and for a long time afterward, she couldn't stand or put weight on the mended leg. Not moving her body led to weight gain, heart problems, depression, and a list of other complications. Her depression was ever-present, and it was hard for her to lift her mood. In the end, she died far too early.

My mother was the exact opposite of my sister. She knew something about moving her body. I recall driving up to her house when my mother was in her later years. There I found her hunkered down in the corner of her yard. She had sweat beading down her lined face, and there was a boulder the size of a watermelon at her knees.

"What are you doing?" I asked.

Her eyes danced in excitement as she replied, "I move rock." She had rolled the chunk of stone some fifteen feet, from one side of the garden to the other. "Look better here."

A report from the *Archives of Internal Medicine* suggests that people who stay physically active during their leisure hours may be biologically younger than those who prefer the couch. In the active individual, chromosomes in white blood cells are more robust—white blood cells protect you against illness and disease—while inactivity, on the flip side, only hastens cell degradation, a lower white blood cell count, and the aging process.

The Body Helps the Mind

We know that exercise improves heart health, fights disease, optimizes cognitive function, helps maintain weight, and strengthens bones and muscle mass. We also know that movement produces endorphins, hormones that reduce pain and stress and improve mood. These hormones are like natural antidepressants.

When you get up and move, mRNA or messenger RNA increases. The molecules carry genetic information for protein synthesis, and we need protein to build muscle and promote the growth and function of neurons. This helps neuroplasticity, which is the brain's ability to form and reorganize connections. When we learn something new, for example, the brain rewires itself. Also important is BDNF, the brain-derived neurotrophic factor protein, which increases mRNA expression. BDNF is a neurotransmitter modulator important in neuron growth and brain function.

Low levels of BDNF are associated with diseases like

Parkinson's, Huntington's, and Alzheimer's, and not surprisingly, people who are obese or depressive also have low levels of BDNF. A simple way to boost BDNF is through physical exertion. A daily spurt of six minutes of high-intensity activity like jumping jacks, lunges, planks, and running quickly in place can do this.

It cannot be said enough that exercise *does* lift the mood. Many studies have looked at this. In one paper that was published in the journal *JAMA Psychiatry*, researchers reported that physical activity can indeed help reduce the risk of depression. A short vigorous workout or a longer low-intensity activity, like walking, will lighten your spirits. Blood flow and oxygen to the brain increase and trigger the release of endorphins and serotonin.

Of course, high levels of physical activity can reduce the risk of depression considerably. According to a 2024 study published in *Neuroscience & Biobehavioral Reviews*, these high levels also found that anxiety decreased strikingly.

Moderate workouts are also beneficial. Hobbies such as weeding, planting, and watering are good for muscle strength and cardiovascular health. (Pastimes like ballroom dancing and tai chi are also beneficial.) Plus, you get a double benefit if you plant a vegetable garden, which can promote a healthy diet. Digging your hands into the soil also brings you closer to nature. A 2007 paper published in the journal *Preventive Medicine Reports* showed that dirt digging stirs up microbes and can activate neurons in the brain, producing the hormone serotonin. Time with Mother Earth reduces stress and anxiety. Gardening was my mother's passion, and she put one hundred percent of her body into it almost daily. This is how she savored life and kept her mind alert until she died at the age of ninety-nine.

How to Get Up and Move

It can be hard to get up and move. Sometimes, I would rather sit on the couch and watch TV. Combining mindfulness with physical activity helped me. My husband bought me a brass singing bowl that I bang while I practice morning yoga. Studies have found that yoga is good for heart health, sleep problems, inflammation, stress, mood, and many other ailments. One study in the *Journal of Clinical Psychiatry* found that yoga can even treat moderate-to-severe depression. This, along with present-moment awareness, doubles the benefits. I now do yoga daily for twenty minutes. I find that quieting the mind and trying to wipe away all thoughts while stretching and bending is greatly calming. It's the ultimate mix of mind and body.

It doesn't matter how you move your body; it just matters that you do. To get up and move:

- Set a specific and attainable goal: "I am going to go for a fifteen-minute walk every day at four o'clock." Routine is a foundation for transformation.
- Avoid setting too broad a goal: "I am going to lose fifty pounds."
- Set smaller, more achievable goals: "I am jogging to the store instead of driving."
- Find a workout buddy to stay accountable and on track.

Any number of habits—poor sleep hygiene, an unhealthy diet, smoking, not enough physical activity—can push the body out of sync. Just the act of moving the body improves the heart, the brain, and even mood. A healthy body helps us fight disease and ill health, and an unhealthy body promotes mental distress. Taking care of our bodies will help us fight the mental misery we get stuck in.

Chapter Twelve

Happiness Means Being Here Right Now

I once knew an extremely busy colleague who had every moment of her day scheduled—an early morning jog, shower, coffee with a friend, at the desk before everyone else, lunch with a colleague, the last one to knock off, meet a different colleague right after work, dinner with boyfriend, attend to reports she didn't complete during the day, read the next book club assignment, floss, go to bed. Even her weekends were filled with an endless to-do list—bake a cake for a friend's get-together, work out at the gym, meet a different friend for coffee, and so on.

One day, she collapsed and called me. "I am so busy."

"So, don't be," I replied, not wanting to be apathetic. I was just being honest. I said that she did not have to do everything on her list. I suspect she kept herself so busy because she didn't like where her mind ventured when she wasn't. An undistracted mind can lead a person straight to her inadequacies—not pretty enough, not slim enough, not a good enough friend, not good enough at her job, not making the right relationship choices, or other perceived flaws. Thoughts can swirl inside our heads, making us miserable.

Being busy feels as though we are accomplishing something. However, busyness can be a hamster wheel of stress. It is the antithesis of mindful thought. And as I have learned, being busy does not ultimately shut down the thoughts that are stuck on continual replay.

For many people, busyness is a sign of success and high status. If you're not busy, then you're nobody. This is a typical exchange:

"How are you doing?"

"So busy."

One can only wonder how this hectic state affects a person, and many people managed this frenzied buzzing even during the COVID pandemic. When people are too busy, they do not take in the air they breathe thoughtfully. Living in the present moment is shunted aside and the buzz of internal misgivings runs in an endless loop.

Silvia Bellezza at Columbia Business School, along with Neeru Paharia at Georgetown University, and Anat Keinan at Harvard Business School researched our culture of busyness. They contend that, in many decades past, a life of leisure was the ultimate sign of high status. Doing a whole lot of nothing meant you were something. The researchers investigated this sea change away from leisure by running several studies. In one, they gave a set of subjects a description of a man in his thirties who works long hours and his calendar is always full. The researchers also gave a separate description of the same man who does not work and has a leisurely lifestyle. The participants deemed the busy person of higher status. We often abide by the motto that hard work brings success, and being busy is the key to life. Granted, being engaged with what you are doing does bring life satisfaction, but the idea of busyness just for busyness's sake is something different.

Frankly, resting our feet is foreign to many of us. Nearly half of American workers don't take all the paid time off offered by employers, a 2023 Pew Research survey found, and about 49 percent worry they will fall behind at work, with 43 percent feeling badly that their vacation might mean added duties for co-workers. In addition, many studies, such as one found in *Psychology & Health*, show that people who take vacations have a lower risk of heart disease, plain and simple.

Not taking a needed break has to be the utmost in mindless thinking. A pause from the daily grind affords better health and well-being, both physical and mental; it also promotes creativity and productivity. However, it takes mindfulness to give life a rest. Removing oneself from work allows the mind to wander, and healthy daydreaming is good for problem-solving. When we are not engaged in or thinking about an important task, a little daydreaming about an unrelated topic may help us solve that pesky problem we must work out. In effect, some woolgathering may boost our productivity—as long as woolgathering does not turn into ruminating.

In research published in the *Journal of Happiness Studies*, professors of psychology David Feldman and Diane Dreher of Santa Clara University asked different groups of study subjects to name their important life goals. Their hopes and ambitions included objectives in relationships and work life. The participants engaged in either one hour of daydreaming, a stress management intervention, or neither. A few weeks later, the subjects reported on their life goal progress, and those who participated in just one daydreaming session enjoyed significant headway in their goals compared with subjects in the stress management or control groups.

Doing Nothing Can Amount to Something

Putting up our feet and *not* thinking, according to history and sociology of science researcher Alex Pang and the author of *Rest: Why You Get More Done When You Work Less*, will give us more energy, better ideas, and a life worth living. In his mind, rest is the key to productivity—and staying clear of negative thinking while we rest is essential.

Unfortunately, in this culture, multitasking is a way of life. With devices and screens in our faces at all hours, multitasking has reached a new level, like it's an Olympic sport. Yet, there's a fallacy in thinking that we can perform multiple tasks all at once. Many researchers have looked at the area of attention spans and found just how bad we are at walking while chewing gum, so to speak. Talking on the cell phone while driving is a good example of this. These two activities don't go together, and it's not unlike driving while under the influence. According to the Centers for Disease Control, some 13 percent of motor vehicle accidents in the US involve distracted driving.

There is a small percentage of people who can supertask several endeavors at the same time. According to research from the *Psychonomic Bulletin & Review*, these people are rare at 2.5 percent of the population. The rest of us? We're better off focusing on just one task and then moving on to the next.

This idea of doing many things at once may be an American standard, yet many people around the world have a different view. Parts of Africa, the Caribbean, the Middle East, and South America, among other regions, see idleness much differently.

The siesta, for example, emerged for the simple reason of escaping the hot sun in the middle of the day. Being too busy can lead to imbalance and poor health, foremost in the form of mental disorders like anxiety. My dad used to say, *man yi dian* (慢一点), "a little slower." He applied this thinking to every aspect of living. He felt that the pace of work and home life should be thoughtful and deliberate. What is the problem with getting *less* done?

This doesn't mean that we have to be slow at our tasks, however. When my brother folds a tray of dumplings, for example, his skill and practice allow him to move at a quick pace. I've likewise watched my cousins prepare dumpling soup, and within ten minutes, they have folded hundreds of dumplings each the size of a walnut. They chat, chuckle, and gossip breezily while their fingers work briskly to get the job done. It's a different kind of busy.

Devices Bring Chaos to the Mind

Our noisy devices add to the clutter and chaos inside our minds. The smartphone does not give the mind a rest with all its beeps. The same pinging happens across the world because everyone is on TikTok, WhatsApp, and WeChat. People everywhere are slaves to their devices, from the young to the old, and we are less inclined to disengage from them.

This need to engage with the smartphone could signal mindless thinking. We have to let go. Yet, to let go, we have to first engage in mindfulness. In a study from the journal *Computers in Human Behavior*, researchers find that people may see their smart devices as "compensatory attachment objects," something like the childhood teddy bear. Most people, on average, keep their phones within reach at virtually all hours, and they also suffer anxiety when separated from their devices. This makes sense because we see the phone as a connection to family, friends, colleagues, and others.

Research in the *Journal of Applied Research in Memory and Cognition* examined whether young people are as addicted to their phones as we think they are. Psychologists deployed methods of inquiry normally used in drug and alcohol addiction studies. The researchers asked subjects if they would choose to reply immediately to their friends who texted them and be paid five dollars or choose to wait and reply an hour later and be paid one hundred dollars. The subjects chose less cash, opting to text now and pass on monetary gain. This may be because money loses value over time, while information loses value in minutes.

It's Okay to Miss Out

It's easy to feel the effects of FOMO, the fear of missing out, during this age of social media. We find out through Instagram that a group of friends got together without us, which makes us feel like a loser as we sit at home alone in a mental tussle with our not-so-social media. Plenty of studies have been done on the topic of this fear. Researchers for a study published in the journal *Motivation and Emotion* had university student subjects fill out surveys to measure their well-being. The students suffered the fear of missing out on social media more at the end of the day, as well as at the end of the week. This fear was also associated with stress, poor sleep, exhaustion, and other difficulties.

The torment of the digital screen and its ambient blue light make these matters worse. I know I'm not supposed to peek at my smartphone before tucking myself in at night, but I sometimes do it anyway. What exactly am I missing out on? According to the journal *Environmental Health Perspectives*, light resets our circadian rhythm. Exposure to artificial light is a sleep disruptor, but short-wavelength blue light may be even more harmful. Blue light may mess with our melatonin production more than other types of light because the body is sensitive to it. Also, what happens when we lie awake after a hit of blue light? We wake up enough for our minds to chew on all the miserable and discouraging thoughts within reach. This is how we undermine our health.

Busyness and thinking too much creates more stress. To stop this cycle, first and foremost, is to know what is important. What do we value? When this happens, many things that we think are important will fall away. A few things to weigh:

- When on vacation, be on vacation. Put a hard stop on work, setting up your out-of-office auto-reply.
- Put aside the to-do list.
- Limit time on social media. You do not need to spend hours scrolling. (A study in the *Journal of Social and Clinical Psychology* found that thirty minutes a day is plenty.)
- Shut off the phone. Better yet, leave it behind.
- If you can't part with the phone, start small. The phone can be left behind at intervals.
- Do nothing and let the mind wander. A place to do this is under a shady tree while watching the clouds.
- Let things go. Nothing needs to be perfect. No one is judging you anyway. And if people are, why are you listening?
- You do not have to be everywhere for everyone. It's

okay to say, "I'm sorry, but I have another commitment." This commitment can be with yourself.

- Are you numbing yourself for a reason? Emotional numbness is a way to ignore what is at the root of your discomfort. It's a good idea to look at what is causing the discomfort, instead of avoiding it.

Getting a handle on busyness is possible. Finding the golden mean in life may help. The golden mean appears in almost every part of living—from sleeping, working, and loving, to imbibing, playing, and much more. A behavior or resource in excess, for example, can tip us to one extreme or the other. The extreme ends of living are unhealthy and negative. We can dial an area of life up or down to reach a healthy equanimity.

The simple act of exercise is a fundamental example. Overdoing fitness or never engaging in it can swing a person into ill health, but aiming for the right amount of physical activity is key. This healthy midpoint applies to other things; everything about us slides along this scale. Our habits, for one, rely on us to stay in balance. If we overeat, we may gain weight. If we eat too little, we may wither away.

Our personality traits are equally reliant on staying steady. It's great to be bold, but excessive fearlessness can turn into daredevil foolishness. Meanwhile, a confident person can morph into an arrogant jerk, and an organized person can become hyperobsessive. And if we labor too much, there's a risk of burning out. On the other end, if we labor too little, we won't have a roof over our heads.

This is also called the Goldilocks Effect—also known as a principle or zone—the early appearance of this term came from

British author and poet Robert Southey in 1837; he wrote the familiar fairy tale *Goldilocks and the Three Bears*. This effect or principle can be applied to our emotions as well, as emotions rely on this same kind of equilibrium. If we banish sadness altogether, we will live outside what is true, and stress needs to be moderated to the right level. Not enough stress means we will be bored out of our minds, and too much stress may bring on anxiety and even panic. Outside this middle zone of "just enough," humility may become insecurity, carefulness may turn into obsessive-compulsiveness, friendliness into obsequiousness, and attentive focus into narrow vision.

It's a Little Little

This idea of *just enough* is like the Hui saying *yi dian dian* (一点 点), a "little little." It's the notion that we should take life a little at a time and not indulge in extremes of behavior, thoughts, and habits. We must balance our moods, from cheerful to gloomy, anxious to mellow. Everything in life is best when stable, steady, and even. Keeping it simple can help. It's a little little.

This applies to materialism as well. Many people would feel out of place living in an expansive mansion with gilded toilets. Living simply—a little little—is preferred by many of us. Certainly, we need enough to live comfortably. Yet what is comfortable exactly? Being driven by the dollar can be an exercise in mindlessness. "I must own that villa in Portofino." "I must buy that Ferrari Monza." This desire feeds negative thinking and general musterbating.

What's more, money can only buy happiness up to a point, and science backs this up. We're better off investing in experiences, instead of collecting material goods. Elizabeth Dunn, a psychology professor at the University of British Columbia, and Michael Norton, a psychology professor at Harvard Business School, are coauthors of the book *Happy Money: The Science of Happier Spending.* They have studied people and their spending habits in myriad ways. They found that in a group of cohorts when asked what made them happier—experiences or material goods—37 percent said they were happier buying material objects, and 57 percent said they were happier engaging in experiences. Studies show that we won't remember the shoes we bought last month, but we will remember stargazing during that meteor shower—and peering at the night sky costs nothing.

I know this from personal experience. My parents did not waste money. They had fled from Communism with the clothes on their backs. They spent ten hard years in Hong Kong living in a Buddhist temple, a cave, and a cleaned-out rabbit hutch. My mother had to walk two and a half miles to the bus to shop for supplies, and it took her an entire day. What mattered more than the hardship, however, was hunger. My sister used to say that she and Brother Number One were shorter than me and Brother Number Two because they had too little to eat during the years right after fleeing the homeland. Most of our forebearers came to this country fleeing some kind of persecution or other hardship. This sort of hardship puts us in a practical frame of mind throughout the rest of our lives.

When We Desire More

The tendency to compare ourselves to others can be set on replay within the mind. "I am not good enough." "I am not successful enough." This comparison can start at a young age. Kids are aware of who has more and who has less. When my boys were little, they came home shouting, "The Worthingtons have a TV in every room." I piped back, "Don't get used to it."

Later, when one of my sons graduated high school, he questioned my decision to settle in our neighborhood. He, for example, got tired of hitching rides in Mercedes SUVs from moms married to hedge fund dads. I used to tell my boys that they could walk instead.

Of course, social psychologists have studied the experience of having less in a pond of more. People who live in a neighborhood where the average household income is higher than theirs feel the discrepancy. According to the research of Robert Frank, a professor of management and economics at Cornell University as well as the author of *The Darwin Economy: Liberty, Competition, and the Common Good*, we compare ourselves with those who are nearby. We see the disparity daily and feel uncomfortable and less worthy if a neighbor has a pool and tennis court. And as far as neighborhoods go, if we made $100,000 a year, we would rather live in a town where others made $80,000, not the other way around.

It's hard to be impervious to social comparisons. People compare, whether they mean to or not. My sister liked to say that when people talk about who has more, we don't have to listen. She was onto something. Tuning out this unnecessary noise is wise; otherwise, the comparisons invade the mind.

It's shameful to be looked down upon, and social comparison is something we can't run from. We are always looking around to see where we land. We smile when we appear better off than others and frown when we appear less well off than others. Yet comparing ourselves to others can put us in a perpetually bleak frame of mind.

Much of our comparisons happen on social media—a schoolmate got married and is pregnant, a colleague got that coveted promotion, or a rival lost twenty pounds. It's easy to feel like a slug. Online networking may well be the beginning and the end of us. We may want to consider a few things:

- Unplug and limit the time you spend scrolling online.
- Unfollow and mute people who make you feel miserable.
- You can use the comparisons as motivating factors. But the only person you can compete with is yourself.
- The social media posts that make you feel crummy are highlight reels. These posts are not the sum of a person's life.
- Don't let these comparisons invade your thoughts.

Prune Your Life Just Enough

Now that my kids are grown, I fantasize about giving away *all* our belongings, buying a beat-up hippie van, stuffing a mattress in it, and driving off—it doesn't even matter where we go. Owning nothing, being free, and not being a slave to the dollar has great appeal. Many people imagine this scenario, and quite a few people live it. I feel that pruning myself might just unload my mind.

Along the esplanade in Pacific Beach, San Diego, a formerly practicing physician has been found gliding on a pair of rollerblades. John Kitchin, nicknamed SloMo, gave up his monied life, walked away from his house and fancy car, and found a tiny apartment to live a simple existence. The gliding former physician tapped into something. It's a philosophy that embraces the real meaning of life, not the worship of material goods.

Fortunately, frugal living is having a moment. Owning less essentially frees the mind. Modern-day Spartans shun consuming more than what is needed. They don't throw food away, refurbish items from socks to furniture, and never buy new when used is just as good.

We have to admire households that are free of *stuff*. These people do not hoard and collect. They don't harbor tchotchkes and knick-knacks, they keep things simple and efficient, and they practice this aesthetic innately. Essentially, physical clutter adds to mental busyness and internal chaos. When things are jumbled in our environment, things are often jumbled inside our heads—all of which can feed the mental loops we suffer.

A study in the *Journal of Environmental Psychology* found that having too many things *can* clutter one's thinking; this confusion renders a person cognitively hampered, bringing on unhappy thoughts. One study presented at a 2001 American Economic Association meeting showed that children raised in a clean and tidy home have a leg up on educational and career success later in life. (Somehow, this nifty information is often lost on kids.)

The brother of a friend of mine died at the age of fifty-six. This brother had no spouse or kids, so my friend arranged his funeral and managed loose ends, including what to do with the brother's many possessions. The brother didn't own a home, jewels, or fat bank account, but he did store old magazines, newspaper clippings, kitchen gadgets, clothes that were too big, and shoes that were too small. It was a prodigious archive that no one wanted. In the end, it pained my friend. While the belongings were important to the deceased brother, there was no action to be taken other than dumping the stuff.

Noted in a 2010 paper published in the journal *Behavior Research and Therapy*, hoarding is strangely, or maybe not so strangely, linked to obsessive compulsiveness. Randy Frost, a professor at Smith College and the author of *Stuff: Compulsive Hoarding and the Meaning of Things*, has studied the hoarding tendencies of older adults and reported that symptoms are often highlighted in late life. Apparently, we hoard more as we age.

Clearing out stuff can be managed throughout life, not just in old age. When I looked in my closet recently, I found items I had not worn in five years. And who were the people in some of the photographs in the shoebox? Owning so much useless stuff *does* clutter my mind.

In Swedish, decluttering is also called *döstädning*, *dö* meaning "death," and *städning* meaning "cleaning." Margareta Magnusson's book, *The Gentle Art of Swedish Death Cleaning*, shares the idea that we shouldn't saddle our loved ones with mountains of stuff after we die. It's painful enough to grieve a loved one's passing, but the agony of going through someone else's clutter can make it worse.

We could all benefit from being a little Swedish by doing the following:

- Start now, not later, and clear out the detritus. Do you really need twenty of one item?
- Focus on what is simple. Getting rid of the no-brainer items will motivate you.
- If there are too many items of the same use, assess the value of each.
- Ask yourself whether someone will want this item

when you die. (Seriously.) I will argue that *no one* will want it.

- Offloading unnecessary belongings—both mental and physical—can help us balance our well-being. It can help us find the flow of life, an age-old concept found in every corner of the world. For the Hui, flow or balance is *qi* (气), the Hindu call it *prana*, the Japanese call it *ki*, and for the Native Americans it's the Great Spirit. Of course, for the Jedi, it's The Force.

Flow is a mainstay in mental well-being. Finding flow in life is hard when:

- We desire physical things.
- We do not know how to let go.
- We can't put down the phone.
- We don't know how to rest or sleep.
- We don't know how to break from our mental loops.

Flow could be a way to gain more mental agility and openness. It may put aside the penchant for negativity.

I remember my dad clearing the table to set it with paper, a brush, an ink stick, a grinding stone, and a cup of water to practice calligraphy. He'd add a bit of water to the stone, and then grind the stick of ink into it. He followed the protocol of holding the stick between his thumb, index, and middle fingers, then moved the stick using a circular motion. He had to have just enough water because the ink had to be the right consistency—too much ink, it would be thick, and too little ink, it would be thin.

A huge part of the exercise was learning how to handle and

care for the ink, brush, and stone. Dad also held the bamboo brush between three fingers, but holding it too high would produce weak strokes, and holding it too close to the bristles gave the user no room to maneuver. Plus, he never rested his elbows on the table, which would have been plain lazy. The process was a mindful foray into the *flow state.* Anyone who understands the art of calligraphy understands the art of flow.

The flow state is the feeling of total engagement in an activity that can take us outside of our heads and ourselves. The painter finds himself in the flow or the zone when he paints, and the mathematician feels the same when solving an equation. The late psychologist Mihaly Csikszentmihalyi, who coined the term *flow,* found that immersing oneself in an engaging pursuit can shift time and space.

Flow is altogether mindful and meditative.

I have friends who enjoy knitting and needlework. They lose themselves in the purls, and their inner chatter disappears. Being one with the flow means you are fully present in this moment, and your worries fall away as you are absorbed in whatever you're doing. This fluid feeling can be applied to numerous tasks. Just think of the pianist looking euphoric in the middle of a concerto or the athlete feeling the runner's high. I like to string together beads with wire, and I become engrossed in its simple beauty.

Likewise, the task of writing can also induce the flow state. Some novelists say they dip into a trance-like state and have little control over their plots. The late novelist Mary Higgins Clark once told me, "My characters end up writing themselves. I have no control over them."

Writing and journaling, in and of itself, boast myriad health benefits. James Pennebaker is a professor emeritus of psychology at the University of Texas and the author of books about the benefits of writing including *Opening Up: The Healing Power of Expressing Emotions*. He found that writing about one's experiences boosts health and wellness; he and many other researchers have studied the positive effects of expressive writing, where pouring out your emotions has a cathartic effect.

You can even find the flow state during sex. Research that was published in the *Journal of Sex & Marital Therapy* found that the state of flow can be experienced while lovemaking. The study examined long-term couples and found that low sexual desire does not have to be a *fait accompli* and that the prognosis for passionate intimacy can be positive. While low libido is nothing new, the rhythm of sex can help. Rhythmic sex can guide and enhance the brain's neural oscillations, which is also known as neural entrainment—this is a trance-like state that taps the subconscious like it is drug-induced.

The flow state is associated with decreased activity in the prefrontal cortex—the part of the brain where memory and reflective consciousness reside. During the experience of the flow state, the prefrontal cortex temporarily deactivates, and a feeling of time distortion takes over. Because curiosity is heightened during this state, the science of flow may also be related to the brain's dopamine reward circuitry.

While the state of flow has been studied in the creative process, you can apply this to everyday living—whereby one remains in the flow of daily life. In effect, flow is everywhere. This touches on mindful living, where you are mindful of inner harmony as you go about your day.

It's easy to ruminate and think about the past, as well as fret over the future, yet it doesn't have to be that way. Letting life happen as it unfolds is a positive way to think. Why should we stress over life when it does not behave? Let's face it, life happens the way it happens, and going with the flow makes sense.

Many people who work with their hands know something about being in the *zone* of flow, and this handy work has an effect, where unconsciousness moves readily—for example, while kneading dough or digging in the garden soil. My mother taught me how to fold a dumpling, and my relatives have shown me their elaborate embroideries, all done by hand.

Using the hands has added benefits beyond the flow effect. Kelly Lambert, a professor of behavioral neuroscience at the University of Richmond and the author of *Lifting Depression: A Neuroscientist's Hands-On Approach to Activating Your Brain's Healing Power*, studied rats that clawed their way to food, as well as rats that were given food with no effort on their part. She found that the working rats fared better and were healthier. Using one's hands releases feel-good neurotransmitters.

My dad's practice of calligraphy had this same effect.

How to Reach the State of Flow

There are a few things that need to happen to create a flow state:

- You have a task you are capable of doing.
- The task must be challenging, not boring.
- Yet the task can't be too challenging or anxiety-inducing.
- You need an end goal.

- You can focus on the task.
- You become immersed in the task.
- You feel a sense of control and mastery.
- You lose a sense of time and space.

The Flow of Nature and Awe

Spending time in nature is another way to get us out of our heads. There is always a lotus flower in stories about the Buddha. This flower, the *lian hua* (蓮花), surfaces through muddy waters, and its waxy petals deflect the dirty muck. It is pure and resilient. This is supposed to be a metaphor, as the Buddha has no desires and is transcendent and peaceful, even in the muck.

My paternal grandfather embraced nature. He thrived in the mountain air, spending more time in the hills than at the hearth. He walked miles and miles trading his goods. He was a prosperous salesman and even bought a second home in the hills, where he shared well water with one of his neighbors, who turned out to be the family of the Fourteenth Dalai Lama. At one point, the family worried that he needed a helper. The teenage boy they hired, however, couldn't keep up with Grandpa, so the old man sat the boy on the donkey while he walked. Grandpa remained in robust health for most of his life by walking and surrounding himself with trees, mountains, and fresh air.

The German social psychologist Erich Fromm first used the term "biophilia," for our attraction to living things. American biologist Edward O. Wilson popularized this idea in his book of the same name, *Biophilia*. In effect, we are genetically and evolutionarily predisposed to all things living, just as the Buddha had a penchant for the lotus.

By just sitting in nature and looking at the trees, we can get out of our minds and feel the flow of life. Communing with nature and taking in its awe-filled splendor is good for your *qi*. The Hui refer to it as the vital life that keeps you balanced and moving forward. Nature even changes your brain for the better.

Research that was published in the journal *Molecular Psychiatry* shows that the amygdala, the part of the brain that processes fear and stress, is less activated in people who live in rural areas. In this study, participants walked for an hour either in a forest or a traffic-filled shopping street in Berlin, Germany. Activity in the amygdala decreased after the walk in the forest.

Another paper published in *Scientific Reports* cited a Monitor of Engagement with the Natural Environment Survey, which included self-reports on health and well-being by nearly 20,000 subjects. It found that a person can feel the benefits of nature in just 120 minutes a week.

According to social psychologist Gregory Bratman, the director of the Environment & Well-Being Lab at the University of Washington, blood flow in the subgenual prefrontal cortex is high when we sit and stew over the small infractions of life, but embracing the awe of nature can remedy and lower the heat of that stew. Nature reminds us that the world is magnificent.

If you are fretting over one anxiety or another, the awe of something as grand as a chiseled mountain peak or a ring of redwoods can give you perspective—one that you need. This is a way to banish self-absorption, the negativity inside your head, and the fixed beliefs of what you think ought to be.

Researchers have studied the effects of spending time in

nature. They wanted to know what "forest bathing" does to people. Forest bathing is called *shinrin-yoku* in Japanese, meaning to take in a forest environment, a term coined by the Japanese Ministry of Agriculture, Forestry and Fisheries in 1982. In a study published in the journal *Environmental Health and Preventive Medicine*, researchers conducted field experiments in forest settings, as well as urban ones, in Japan. Half the participants walked in a forest; the other half walked in an urban area. Afterward, participants swapped environments. The researchers found that walking in a forest setting lowered cortisol, pulse rate, blood pressure, and sympathetic nerve activity.

Tending to the Garden

We don't have to trek in the Tibetan plateaus, like Grandpa, to welcome the advantages of nature. Even tending an indoor garden can boost our mental health. Likewise, according to the *International Journal of Environmental Research and Public Health*, having potted plants or even fresh flowers can offer health gains as well. In one study, plants were added to a set of work offices and not others, and the subjects who worked in an office with a plant performed better in tasks that called for attention and concentration.

The joy of horticulture is practiced worldwide. My mother may have had the greenest thumb out of everyone I knew. Her specialty was the rose bush. When I was growing up, she had every color imaginable, red, white, orange, and a violet that was close to black. Neighbors stopped by when she was in the front garden clipping and weeding. They asked, "How do you do it?" "Flower need food," she would reply, and she wasn't being flippant. She pointed at literal food scrapings, like eggshells and spent tea leaves at the foot of each bush. Even into her nineties, Mom coaxed her plants to bloom. Those plants have done their work by keeping her alive for as long as they did.

In another study published in the *Journal of Personality and Social Psychology*, subjects climbed the University of California, Berkeley clock tower and peered out over the bay, the Golden Gate Bridge, and the city of San Francisco. Meanwhile, the control subjects of the study looked around the inside of the tower. The subjects who took in the view of the bay felt less stress than the control group. When we look out toward the trees and the sky, and not in, our day-to-day grievances and petty annoyances fade, and we live better lives, ones with meaning, ones without the noise inside our heads.

We know that nature and its trees and plants and animals are good for us, but some of us are hard-pressed to find green trees when the concrete city is where we must be. But we do not have to travel to Greenland to see the aurora borealis to get the benefits of nature and the feeling of awe. You can get that benefit by swimming in a mountain lake over a weekend jaunt, hiking in nearby hills or a local nature preserve or an urban wildlife sanctuary. You can also get that benefit by sitting under a tree in a city park in short stints throughout the week or potting plants for your windowsill.

Savor Life

People who embrace nature also know how to savor life. They soak up positive emotions, focus on the present, put away distractions, disengage with worry, enjoy a meal slowly, smell the flowers, and generally are mindful. Here are some methods of savoring:

Savor the present. When we stop to look around us with intention, we can savor the moment and disengage from the noisy mind. What we see, hear, smell, and touch matter. Once, in Hawaii, I was standing on a ridge, and I looked down to see a rainbow. It was a perfect circle. I stopped and stared at it until it disappeared. I was in awe. No wonder a full rainbow is called a *glory*. For days after this, I kept telling my friends what I had seen. In a way, sharing this had extended the feelings of magnificence.

Savor the past. Thinking about something joyful that happened does not mean getting stuck in the past. It just means feeling happy about something that happened. It's when you think about a past moment when you felt elated. A while back, the orthopedic surgeon showed me my MRI results and announced that I didn't need shoulder surgery. Walking home, I was practically singing with exuberance for life. I can even think back to that feeling and dip into it.

Try anticipatory savoring. Expecting a certain outcome can lead to disappointment. It's easy to think about an upcoming event and expect a list of things to happen and not happen. "I am going to cook an amazing souffle" (the dish looks like a crater). "My guests will be entertained by my funny friend" (the friend comes down with the flu). Instead, we can anticipate a happy occasion without setting up our expectations.

We want to be busy and diverted because the undistracted mind reminds us of our inadequacies. Sometimes we want to look busy to seem important. But when we do this, we are not being mindful or thoughtful.

Instead, we can live in the flow of life. We can shut off our phones, take a real vacation, and let the mind be idle. The flow state takes us out of our heads. Flow is mindful and thoughtful. It allows us to savor life, soak up positivity, and embrace the present.

Chapter Thirteen

What Do We Value?

The common question, "What do you do?" is frequently asked at cocktail parties and always feels strange to me. Certainly, work and careers are important. I want to do the best I can and like the feeling that I am giving my utmost effort. Accolades for a job well done are great, but I think that as long as I am doing my best, that, in itself, is fulfilling. Engagement in work is only a part of what gives us purpose.

I wonder what would happen if the person we're talking to at the party would rather chat about how much he loves his family, an enlightening book he's reading, or a hobby that makes him feel alive. Life seems dependent on our status in society, and how we identify ourselves revolves so much around what we do. *I'm a lawyer, doctor, teacher.* However, worrying about status is harmful to our health and frame of mind, and often thinking about status makes us feel less than adequate. Our inadequacies make us feel low self-worth, insecure, and mediocre. These feelings lead to negative thinking and misery.

In other parts of the world, such a conversation opener is oftentimes food- or family-related, or whether we share a mutual friend. "Did you try the broccoli soaked in garlic sauce?" "Your baby has a sweet smile." "Do you know my neighbor so-and-so?"

When we know what we value, we have clarity and purpose. Knowing our values and what matters is a mainstay of mindful thinking. When we stay focused on what matters to us, the chaff falls away.

The late social psychologist Milton Rokeach developed the Rokeach Value Survey to help classify values in business organizations, and it is used by career counselors, clinical therapists, and many others. The Michigan State University professor included different terminal and instrumental values in his scale. Terminal values are the desired goals we want to achieve in life including happiness, friendship, love, wisdom, and self-respect. Instrumental values help us accomplish these terminal values. Here are some examples of how they work:

- The instrumental values of forgiveness and honesty can help us reach the terminal value of mature love.
- The instrumental values of independence and curiosity can help us achieve the terminal value of happiness.
- The instrumental values of conscientiousness and perseverance can help us realize the terminal value of accomplishment.

People in leadership positions use terminal and instrumental values to help guide their organizations to success. For example, when an employee is open and ambitious, it may lead to professional growth. Meanwhile, when an employee takes responsibility and accountability for their actions, it may lead to honesty and integrity for themselves and their institution.

Physician Nina Cerfolio learned what she values and what matters in life. The professor of medicine at Mount Sinai in New York, and the author of *Psychoanalytic and Spiritual Perspectives on Terrorism: Desire for Destruction*, discovered what is vital through a difficult period of physical and mental suffering. In 2005, she traveled to Chechnya, a war-torn region not unlike Ukraine, to help the injured and wounded. She spent ten days in a country that needed skilled physicians. During that time, a Russian Federal Security Service agent escorted her and other professionals—people like her who wanted to help others. At one point, the Russian agent handed her a beer.

Cerfolio did not know why she later suffered flu-like symptoms such as nausea, vomiting, and dizziness. She suspected the beer contained anthrax. What had seemed like a friendly gesture had turned into a malignant act. She returned to New York in ill health that lasted for three years. This meant recurring pneumonia, infections, chronic inflammation, and other problems.

Cerfolio realized she could easily be bitter, disengaged, and pessimistic about this experience, but instead, she turned to openness, positivity, and compassion. She also slowed down and accepted her life just as it was. As a result, she became more connected with herself, and after she returned to work, she became more connected with her patients. Perhaps the poisoning helped her to find her authentic self.

We realize we can stop the cycle of negative thinking by being fluid, open, and mindful just like Cerfolio. Flexibility of thought means the acceptance of all negative states. Fluid, open thinking embraces all emotions—happiness and sadness, serenity and anxiety, anger and humor. Our mood states are fine as is. We do not have to be set in one way of thinking. Cerfolio felt that she learned the core meaning of life, and this is something most older people have come to understand.

The meaning and purpose of life sit squarely in the domain of philosophy, which can sometimes border on psychology. Confucius, Plato, and other philosophers had much to say about what is important in life. Their tenets are simple:

- Be decent and live with peace and harmony.
- Revere parents and be kind to elders.
- Find humanity within and cherish the heart.
- Live with honesty and trustworthiness.
- Be respectful of everyone.
- Do the right thing.
- Work hard.
- Contemplate life over seeking material wealth and power.
- Help others, especially those in need.

We can take stock of what has meaning and purpose for *us*, and we do so at certain points in our time on Earth. Midlife is often one of those points. The kids are in college, our work life is more than half over, and we start to wonder, *Am I content?*

In many cultures, there is little fuss over this stage of life. Some researchers contend that the so-called "midlife crisis" is a cultural construct in Euro-American societies. The book *Welcome to Middle Age!: (And Other Cultural Fictions)* is filled with essays by social scientists arguing that middle age does not exist. The authors, including Richard Shweder, the book's editor and a professor of human development at the University of Chicago, contend that across the globe in non-Euro-American societies, mature adulthood is appreciated and privileged. Men in these societies are less enamored with the red sports car, and women don't have angst over hormone replacement therapy, sagging breasts, or squeezing into size-two jeans. Other cultures are less obsessed with youth than the West. However, the world *is* becoming more digitally connected, and the Western view of youth and middle age may be infiltrating other regions.

On a trip to the homeland, extended family members I had not seen for thirty-five years greeted me and my mom. They all ran past me to welcome my nonagenarian mom first. Any other reaction would have been impolite. She was the eldest in the room and had a gaggle of people around her. The younger folk asked her many questions: "What was life like in the old days?" "How can I live to be as old as you?" Everyone fawned over my mom like she was royalty.

Watching a senior hold forth with all her wisdom is a fine thing to witness. If we're in our golden years, we should be allowed to talk as much as we want. In many parts of the world, being elderly affords many life vouchers. The Hui also revere and honor their dead. We talk to and hope that our ancestors will hear and guide us in some way. They are, ultimately, founts of wisdom that bestow meaning and purpose on us.

The elders I know say they wished they knew, when they were younger, what they know now. *Why had I been so upset about things that happened when I was young?* From their vantage point of old age, it's not worth getting upset or having negative thoughts about the many things that seem unsettling. I see what they are saying, and they are right. Living a good life takes a certain emotional maturity. It's a maturity that helps a person maintain a positive perspective. I want to be a wise elder. We should all emulate the wisdom of these important members of our tribe.

The Wisdom of Old Age

In her elderly years, my mom wasn't too concerned about wrinkles. She had so much enthusiasm for her flowers that it was all-consuming. One morning, Mom urgently called my sister, "I want new bush. I ready. I waiting. Where you?" Her shoes and bag were lined up at the door for a quick departure. Mom picked out two bushes at the nursery. She brought the plants home and staged the pots where they were to be planted. That afternoon she decided that the placement of the bushes wasn't right, and she moved them from one part of her garden to another, over and over again. I marveled that my elderly mother could carry the pots at all. Her roses and other flowers gave her life meaning and purpose.

Elderly people know something about life's meaning and purpose. Karl Pillemer, a professor of human development and gerontology at Cornell University and the author of *30 Lessons for Living: Tried and True Advice from the Wisest Americans*, believes in mining the wisdom of elders. He has surveyed octogenarians and folks even older, and he found that they can give us solid lessons for life because they have lived it.

Pillemer's research has shown that many seniors have lived through extreme life events—poverty, war, and illness, among many other traumas. In my mother's case, she watched her father die of a heart attack after the Japanese bombed their village. My parents also had to flee their homeland when Communism came.

After that, they planted and lived on papayas and bananas for a long time. They gained experience by living through real hardship.

In his book, Pillemer offers the following advice about seeking counsel from elders:

- Find someone to interview, one you want to emulate as an older person.
- This person should be in their seventies or even older.
- A person any younger wouldn't have the span of years, experientially speaking.
- A younger person may not be able to comment on a long view of life.
- This wise individual should resemble how you see yourself in the future.

Thinking Based in Reality

When we're negative, we're not open; we're stuck in a rigid headspace. It's a perfect mindset for defeating the self, as well as a mental trap often found in defeatist thinking—the person who loses his job immediately opines that his life has been ruined. Everything has been destroyed, and that is the case forever. However, he feels he is being reasonable in his view. All areas of life are affected—intimacy, work, health, and friendship.

In general, gloomy thinking is not based in reality. The negative person is reproachful toward herself and also demands quite a lot from others. Negative thinking can also lead to mood disorders like stress, depression, and anxiety; in extreme cases, it can even bring on suicidal thoughts. During the pandemic, according to the CDC, loneliness, anxiety, and depression rose, especially in young people. These types of thoughts hamper a person's decision-making and problem-solving abilities, as well as overall well-being.

It feels like we have been in a wave of communal negativity. Modern-day chaos is entrenched right now. There is so much we have had to, and will continue to, contend with. Life has been and will be tricky; we have had pandemics, inequality, division, burnout, war, climate change, the fear of being deported, disasters both natural and manmade, and general societal misgivings. These things won't just go away, and there are difficulties yet to come.

The Mind in Full Circle

Understanding our life's priorities like a wise elder is essential. Psychologist Steven Hayes's evidence-based acceptance and commitment therapy is based on this foundation. This type of therapy encourages us to know what we value. For me, I want to do my best in my work life, but even more important to me is my family.

Now that I'm remarried, I have a big, messy flock of five grown kids plus their significant others. At first, I didn't think the triumphs, struggles, and worries of such an extended network would affect me to any great degree. I was wrong. I do think about each family member with complete protectiveness. I feel outraged when one has been wronged, and I am joyful when another is exuberant. I'm grateful because I could have ended up with extended family dysfunction instead.

Still, my husband and I have to engineer the cohesion of our network. At one point, we rented a large vacation house for all of us. We swam in the river, rode bikes in the woods, played board games and charades, cooked, and ate a lot throughout the week. We even invited my ex-husband, who is a most good-natured participant. Getting together like this makes up the happiest times of my life. Friends and family make me happy, and I never feel alone. Remembering what I value has set me free from the negative loops inside my head. I have learned that there is no one way to think and be.

I want to do the best I can in life. Doing my best at work is important to me, but doing my best for my family and loved ones is even more crucial. This is what I value, and it's my beacon. Our wise elders know this about life. Knowing what has meaning and purpose keeps our minds steady, and this is at the core of contentment. The elders we know have a tap on meaning and purpose, and we can learn from that knowledge. Older people can give us solid lessons for living because they have lived it. Our priorities are at the foundation of a grounded life. What we value will set us free from the negativity we suffer. The moral of this story is that the mind's default to negativity is not a *fait accompli*. Knowing what we value changes so much.

Acknowledgments

Thanks to Seth Gillihan for introducing me to Rick Bleiweiss, both of whom have been generous and open. Much appreciation goes to Candice Roditi, Alenka Linaschke, Kathryn English, Holly Rubino, Courtney Vatis, Lysa Williams, Josie Woodbridge, and the kind and patient editor Windy Goodloe, among many others. In addition, the sublime illustrations in each chapter were drawn by Hamil Ma.

I must mention how much I value everyone at *Psychology Today*, especially Jo Colman, who has not fired me yet.

Friends and family are, of course, most central in my life. This includes diasporas of beloved others in nearly every continent—Bittner, Middelmann, Ma, Eid, anyone married in or out, and otherwise connected. I also appreciate my book club, a monthly gathering that pushes me to read titles I would never pick up.

My sons, daughters, bonus kids, and annexed others are

a giant joy. This egalitarian shout-out must be in alphabetical order backward—Zak, Monica, Matthew, Luise, KC, Jessie, Elizabeth, David, Chelsea, Carl, and Amiel. I am also married to the most loving and patient man who dotes on me even though he knows I am quite capable. I am in love every day.

Bibliography

Introduction

World Health Organization. "COVID-19 pandemic triggers 25% increase in prevalence of anxiety and depression worldwide: Wake-up call to all countries to step up mental health services and support." Updated March 2022. https://www.who.int/news/item/02-03-2022-covid-19-pandemic-triggers-25-increase-in-prevalence-of-anxiety-and-depression-worldwide.

Chapter 1: We Are Miserable by Default

Adam-Troian, Jais, Eric Bonetto, Thomas Arciszewski. "Using absolutist word frequency from online searches to measure population mental health dynamics." *Scientific Reports* 12, Issue 1 (2022): 2619. https://doi.org/10.1038/s41598-022-06392-4.

Arthur, Shaw, Victor H. Mair. "East Asian Historical Traditions of Well-Being." The Pursuit of Human Well-Being. *International Handbooks of Quality-of-Life*. (2017): 59–82. https://doi.org/10.1007/978-3-319-39101-4_3.

Baumeister, Roy F., Ellen Bratslavsky, Catrin Finkenauer, Kathleen D. Vohs. "Bad Is Stronger Than Good." *Review of General Psychology* 5, No. 4 (2001): 323-370. https://doi.org/10.1037/1089- 2680.5.4.323.

Boehm, J., Christopher Peterson, Mika Kivimaki, Laura Kubzansky. "A prospective study of positive psychological well-being and coronary heart disease." *Health Psychology 30, No. 3* (2011): 259-267. https://doi.org/10.1037/a0023124.

Brickman, Phillip, Donald T. Campbell. "Hedonic Relativism and Planning the Good Society." Adaptation-level theory: a symposium (1971): 287-305. https://api.semanticscholar.org/CorpusID:140481039.

De Vaus, June, Matthew J. Hornsey, Peter Kuppens, Brock Bastion. "Exploring the East-West Divide in Prevalence of Affective Disorder: A Case for Cultural Differences in Coping With Negative Emotion." *Personality and Social Psychology Review* 22, No. 3 (2017): 285-304. https://doi.org/10.1177/1088868317736222.

Ellis, Albert, PhD. How to Control Your Anxiety Before it Controls You. Citadel, 2016.

Ford, Brett Q., Julia O. Dmitrieva, Daniel Heller, et al. "Culture shapes whether the pursuit of happiness predicts higher levels of well-being." *Journal of Experimental Psychology*: General 144, No. 6 (2015): 1053-1062. https://doi.org/10.1037/xge0000108.

Gainsburg, Izzy, Ethan Kross. "Distanced self-talk changes how people conceptualize the self." Journal of Experimental Social Psychology 88 (2020): 103969. https://doi.org/10.1016/j.jesp.2020.103969.

Geher, Glenn, PhD. "Darwin's Bucket List: It's Not About Swimming With Dolphins, Skydiving, or Seeing the Rolling Stones," *Psychology Today* (March 10, 2019) https://www.psychologytoday.com/us/blog/darwins-subterranean-world/201903/darwin-s-bucket-list.

Graham-Engeland, Jennifer E., Nancy L. Sin, Joshua M. Smyth. "Negative and positive affect as predictors of inflammation: Timing matters." *Brain, Behavior, and Immunity* 74 (2018): 222-230. https://doi.org/10.1016/j.bbi.2018.09.011.

Grossman, Igor, Ethan Kross. "Exploring Solomon's Paradox: Self-Distancing Eliminates the Self-Other Asymmetry in Wise Reasoning About Close Relationships in Younger and Older Adults." Sage Journals 25, Issue 8 (2024): 1571-1580. https://doi.org/10.1177/0956797614535400.

Gruber, June, Iris B. Mauss, Maya Tamir. "A Dark Side of Happiness? How, When, and Why Happiness Is Not Always

Good." *Perspectives on Psychological Science 6, No. 3* (2011): 222-233. https://doi.org/10.1177/1745691611406927.

Hilbig, Benjamin E. "Good things don't come easy (to mind): Explaining framing effects in judgments of truth." *Experimental Psychology* 59, No. 1 (2011): 38-46. https://doi.org/10.1027/1618-3169/a000124.

Hilgard, Joseph, Anna Weinberg, Greg Hajcak, Proudfit, Bruce D. Bartholow. "The Negativity Bias in Affective Picture Processing Depends on Top-Down and Bottom-Up Motivational Significance." *Emotion 14, No. 5* (2014): 940-949. https://doi.org/10.1037/a0036791.

Ito, T.A., J.T. Larsen, N.K. Smith, J.T. Cacioppo. "Negative information weighs more heavily on the brain: the negativity bias in evaluative categorizations." *Journal of Personality and Social Psychology 75, No. 4* (1998): 887-900. https://doi.org/10.1037//0022-3514.75.4.887.

Karim, Helmet T., Maria Ly, Gary Yu, et al. "Aging faster: worry and rumination in late life are associated with greater brain age." *Neurobiology of Aging 101* (2021): 13-21. https://doi.org/10.1016/j.neurobiolaging.2021.01.009.

Kessler, Ronald C., Evelyn J. Bromet. "The epidemiology of depression across cultures." *Annual Review of Public Health* 34 (2014): 119-138. https://doi.org/10.1146/annurev-publhealth-031912-114409.

Kim, Junhyung, Joon Hee Kwon, Joohan Kim, et al. "The effects of positive or negative self-talk on the alteration of brain functional connectivity by performing cognitive tasks." *Scientific Reports* 11 (2021): 14873. https://doi.org/10.1038/s41598-021-94328-9.

Kross, Ethan, Ozlem Ayduk. "Marking Meaning out of Negative Experiences by Self-Distancing." Current Directions in Psychological Science 20, Issue 3 (2011): 187-191. https://doi.org/10.1177/0963721411408883.

Kross, Ethan. *Chatter: The Voice in Our Head, Why It Matters, and How to Harness It.* Crown, 2021.

Lam, Kent C.H., Roger Buehler, Cathy McFarland, Michael Ross, Irene Cheun. "Cultural Differences in Affective Forecasting: The Role of Focalism." *Personality and Social Psychology Bulletin 31, No. 9* (2005): 1296-1309. https://doi.org/10.1177/0146167205274691.

Layous, K., H. Lee, I. Choi, S. Lyubomirsky. "Culture Matters When Designing a Successful Happiness-Increasing Activity: A Comparison of the United States and South Korea." *Journal of Cross-Cultural Psychology* 44, No. 8 (2013): 1294-1303. https://doi.org/10.1177/0022022113487591.

Luo, Cheng, Qifu Li, Yongxiu Lai, et al. "Altered functional connectivity in default mode network in absence epilepsy: A resting-state fMRI study." Human Brain Mapping 32, Issue 3 (2011): 438-449. https://doi.org/10.1002/hbm.21034.

Lyubomirsky, Sonja. *The How of Happiness: A New Approach to Getting the Life You Want.* Penguin, 2008.

Menon, Vinod. "20 years of the default mode network: A review and synthesis." Neuron 111, Issue 16 (2023): 2469-2487. https://doi.org/10.1016/j.neuron.2023.04.023.Miyamoto,

Yuri, Yukiko Uchida, Phoebe C. Ellsworth. "Culture and mixed emotions: Co-occurrence of positive and negative emotions in Japan and the US." *Emotion* 10, No. 3 (2010): 404-415. https://doi.org/10.1037/a0018430.

Nolen-Hoeksema, Susan. *Women Who Think Too Much: How to Break Free of Overthinking and Reclaim Your Life.* Holt, 2004.

Raichle, Marcus E., Ann Mary MacLeod, Abraham Z. Snyder, William J. Powers, Debra A. Gusnard, Gordon L. Shulman. "A default mode of brain function." PNAS 98, No. 2 (2001): 676-682. https://doi.org/10.1073/pnas.98.2.676.

Rozin, Paul, Edward B. Royzman. "Negativity Bias, Negativity Dominance, and Contagion." *Personality and Social Psychology Review* 5, Issue 4 (2001): 296-320. https://doi.org/10.1207/S15327957PSPR0504_2.

Ruppert, Marina C., Andrea Greuel, Julie Freigang, et al. "The default mode network and cognition in Parkinson's disease: A multimodal resting-state network approach." Human Brain Mapping 42, Issue 8 (2021): 2623-2641. https://doi.org/10.1002/hbm.25393.

Sapolsky, Robert M. *Why Zebras Don't Get Ulcers.* Holt, 2004.

Tierney, John, Roy F. Baumeister. *The Power of Bad: How the Negativity Effect Rules Us, and How We Can Rule It.* Penguin, 2019.

Tversky, Amos and Daniel Kahneman. "Judgment under Uncertainty: Heuristics and Biases: Biases in judgments reveal some heuristics of thinking under uncertainty." *Science* 185, Issue 4157 (1974): 1124-1131. https://doi.org/10.1126/science.185.4157.1124.

Uchida, Yukiko, Vinai Norasakkunkit, Shinobu Kitayama. "Cultural constructions of happiness: theory and empirical evidence." *Journal of Happiness Studies 5, No. 3* (2004): 223-239. https://doi.org/10.1007/s10902-004-8785-9.

Uchida, Yukiko, Yuji Ogihara. "Personal or Interpersonal Construal of Happiness: A Cultural Psychological Perspective." *International Journal of Well-Being 2, No. 4: Special Issue: Happiness: Does Culture Matter?* (2012): 354-369. https://doi.org/10.5502/ijw.v2.i4.5.

Vaish, Amrisha, Tobias Grossman, Amanda Woodward. "Not all emotions are created equal: The negativity bias in social-emotional development." Psychological Bulletin 134, No. 3 (2008): 383-403. https://doi.org/10.1037/0033-2909.134.3.383.

Wang, Huaning, Ling-Li Zeng, Yunchun Chen, Hong Yin, Qingrong Tan, Dewen Hu. "Evidence of a dissociation pattern in default mode subnetwork functional connectivity in schizophrenia." *Scientific Reports 5, Issue 1* (2015): 14655. https://doi.org/10.1038/srep14655.

White, Lawrence T. *Culture Conscious: Briefings on Culture, Cognition, and Behavior.* Wiley, 2020.

Witters, Dan. "U.S. Depression Rates Reach New Highs." *Gallup*, May 17, 2023. https://news.gallup.com/poll/505745/depression-rates-reach-new-highs.aspx.

Yanko, Matthew R. and Thomas M. Spalek. "Driving With the Wandering Mind: The Effect That Mind-Wandering Has on Driving Performance." Human Factors 56, Issue 2 (2013): 260-269. https://doi.org/10.1177/0018720813495280.

Chapter Two: How to Handle the Ambiguity of Life

Chen, Kuan-Hua, Casey L. Brown, Jenna L. Wells, et al. "Physiological linkage during shared positive and shared negative emotion." Journal of Personality and Social Psychology 121, No. 5 (2021): 1029-1056. https://doi.org.10.1037/pspi0000337.

Djikic, Maja, Keith Oatley, Mihnea C. Moldoveanu. "Opening the Closed Mind: The Effect of Exposure to Literature on the Need for Closure." *Creativity Research Journal 25,*

No. 2 (2013): 149-154. https://doi.org/10.1080/10400419.2013.783735.

Ellis, Albert. *The Road to Tolerance: The Philosophy of Rational Behavior Therapy.* Prometheus, 2004.

Friedman, Ron, Edward L. Deci, Andrew J. Elliot, Arlen C. Moller, Henk Aarts. "Motivational synchronicity: Priming motivational orientations with observations of others' behaviors." Motivation and Emotion 34 (2009): 34-38. https://doi.org/10.1007/s11031-009-9151-3.

Fryer, Daniel. "Putting the Fun Back into Dysfunctional: Is the use of humour in Rational Emotive Behaviour Therapy a desirable condition or an amusing aside?" *The Rational Emotive Behaviour Therapist* 14, No. 1 (2011): 63-72. https://www.danielfryer.com/wp-content/uploads/2019/10/DF_dv1_REBT_2011_Publication_Nov_v2.pdf.

Hertel, Paula, Nilly Mor, Chiara Ferrari, Olivia Hunt, Nupur Agrawal. "Looking on the Dark Side: Rumination and Cognitive-Bias Modification." *Clinical Psychological Science 2, Issue 6* (2014): 714-726. https://doi.org/10.1177/2167702614529111.

National Library of Medicine. "Depression." Accessed June 16, 2025. https://medlineplus.gov/genetics/condition/depression/.

Pennebaker, James W., *Opening Up: The Healing Power of Expressing Emotions.* The Guilford Press, 1997.

Sloan, Denise M., Brian P. Marx, Patricia A. Resick, et al. "Effect of Written Exposure Therapy vs Cognitive Processing Therapy on Increasing Treatment Efficiency Among Military Service Members With Posttraumatic Stress Disorder. A Randomized Noninferiority Trial." *JAMA Network Open 5, No. 1* (2022): e2140911. https://doi.org/10.1001/jamanetworkopen.2021.40911.

Tangney, June Price, Jeff Stuewig, Debra J. Mashek. "Moral Emotions and Moral Behavior." *Annual Review of Psychology 58* (2007): 345-372. https://doi.org/10.1146/annurev.psych.56.091103.070145.

Wronska, Marta K., Aleksandra Bujacz, Małgorzata A. Gocłowska, Eric F. Rietzschel, Bernard A. Nijstad. "Person-task fit: Emotional consequences of performing divergent versus convergent thinking tasks depend on the need for cognitive closure." *Personality and Individual Differences 142* (2019): 172-178. https://doi.org/10.1016/j.paid.2018.09.018.

Chapter Three: The Science of Emotions

Brickman, Phillip, Donald T. Campbell. "Hedonic Relativism and Planning the Good Society." Adaptation-level theory: a symposium (1971): 287-305. https://api.semanticscholar.org/CorpusID:140481039.

Chen, Kuan-Hua, Casey L. Brown, Jenna L. Wells, et al. "Physiological linkage during shared positive and shared negative emotion." Journal of Personality and Social Psychology 121, No. 5 (2021): 1029-1056. https://doi.org/10.1037/pspi0000337.

Friedman, Ron, Edward L. Deci, Andrew J. Elliot, Arlen C. Moller, Henk Aarts. "Motivational synchronicity: Priming motivational orientations with observations of others' behaviors." Motivation and Emotion 34 (2009): 34-38. https://doi.org/10.1007/s11031-009-9151-3.

Gilbert, Paul, Sue Procter. "Compassionate Mind Training for People with High Shame and Self-Criticism: Overview and Pilot Study of a Group Therapy Approach." *Clinical Psychology and Psychotherapy 13* (2006): 353-379. https://doi.org/10.1002/cpp.507.

Gross, James J. "The emerging field of emotion regulation: An integrative review." *Review of General Psychology 2, No. 3* (1998) https://doi.org/10.1037/1089-2680.2.3.271.

Leach, Colin Wayne, Atilla Cidam. "When is shame linked to constructive approach orientation? A meta-analysis." *Journal of Personality and Social Psychology 109, No. 6* (2015): 983-1002. https://doi.org/10.1037/pspa0000037.

Lieberman, Matthew D., Naomi Eisenberger, Molly J. Crockett, Sabrina M. Tom, Jennifer H. Pfeifer, Baldwin M. Way.

"Putting feelings into words: Affect labeling disrupts amygdala activity in response to affective stimuli." Psychological Science 18, No. 5 (2007): 421-428. https://doi.org/10.1111/j.1467-9280.2007.01916.x.

National Library of Medicine. "Depression." Accessed June 16, 2025. https://medlineplus.gov/genetics/condition/depression/.

Renna, Megan E., Jean M. Quintero, David M. Fresco, Douglas S. Mennin. "Emotion Regulation Therapy: A Mechanism-Targeted Treatment for Disorders of Distress," *Frontiers in Psychology 8, No. 98* (2017) https://doi.org/10.3389/fpsyg.2017.00098.

Tignor, Stephanie M., C. Randall Colvin. "The Interpersonal Adaptiveness of Dispositional Guilt and Shame: A Meta-Analytic Investigation." *Journal of Personality* 85, No. 3 (2017): 341-363. https://doi.org/10.1111/jopy.12244.

Tsai, Jeanne L., Brian Knutson, Helene H. Fung. "Cultural variation in affect valuation." *Journal of Personality and Social Psychology* 90, No. 2 (2006): 288-307. https://doi.org/10.1037/0022-3514.90.2.288.

Zhang, Heyun, Sisi Chen, Rong Wang, Jiang Jiang, Yan Yu, Huanhuan Zhao. "How Upward Moral Comparison Influences Prosocial Behavioral Intention: Examining the Mediating Role of Guilt and the Moderating Role of

Moral Identity," *Frontiers in Psychology* 8 (2017) https://doi.org/10.3389/fpsyg.2017.01554.

Chapter Four: The Truth About Failure and Self-Sabotage

Al-Mosaiwi, Mohammed, Tom Johnstone. "In an Absolute State: Elevated Use of Absolutist Words Is a Marker Specific to Anxiety, Depression, and Suicidal Ideation." *Clinical Psychological Science 6, No. 4* (2018): 529-542. http://journals.sagepub.com/doi/abs/10.1177/2167702617747074.

Békés, Vera, David M. Dunkley, Geneviève Taylor, et al. "Chronic Stress and Attenuated Improvement In Depression Over 1 Year: The Moderating Role of Perfectionism." *Behavior Therapy 46, No. 4* (2015): 478-492. https://doi.org/10.1016/j.beth.2015.02.003.

Brooks, David. *The Road to Character.* Random House, 2016.

Clance, Pauline Rose, Suzanne Imes. "The Imposter Phenomenon in High-Achieving Women: Dynamics and Therapeutic Intervention." *Psychotherapy: Theory, Research, and Practice* 15, No. 3 (1978): 241-247. https://doi.org/10.1037/h0086006.

Curran, Thomas, Andrew P. Hill. "Perfectionism Is Increasing Over Time: A Meta-Analysis of Birth Cohort Differences From 1989 to 2016." *Psychological Bulletin* 145, No. 4 (2019): 410-429. https://doi.org/10.1037/bul0000138.

Data Pandas. Depression Rates By Country. Updated May 2025. https://www.datapandas.org/ranking/depression-rates-by-country#bottom.

DeSilver, Drew. "What's on your table? How America's diet has changed over the decades." Pew Research (December 2016) http://www.pewresearch.org/fact-tank/2016/12/13/whats-on-your-table-how-americas-diet-has-changed-over-the-decades/.

Dunn, B.D., L. A. Burr, H. B. Smith, et al. "Moods with Detachment: Turning gold into lead: Dampening appraisals reduce happiness and pleasantness and increase sadness during anticipation and recall of pleasant activities." *Behaviour Research and Therapy* (August 2018) https://www.sciencedirect.com/science/article/abs/pii/S0005796718300718?via%3Dihub.

Geher, G. "The Psychology of 'What If': Going back in time, or 'counterfactual' thinking, can have mixed outcomes." *Psychology Today* (September 2018) https://www.psychologytoday.com/us/blog/darwins-subterranean-world/201809/the-psychology-what-if.

Gilbert, Paul, Mark W. Baldwin, Chris Irons, Jodene R. Baccos, Michelle Palmer. "Self-Criticism and Self-Warmth: An Imagery Study Exploring Their Relation to Depression." *Journal of Cognitive Psychotherapy: An International Quarterly* 20, No. 2 (2006): 182-200. https://doi.org/10.1891/jcop.20.2.183.

Gillihan, Seth J., PhD. "Why It's Easy to Procrastinate—and 7 Ways to Break the Habit." *Psychology Today* (blog) 2016. https://www.psychologytoday.com/us/blog/think-act-be/201612/why-its-easy-procrastinate-and-7-ways-break-the-habit.

Grant Study of Adult Development. Harvard. Ongoing. https://www.adultdevelopmentstudy.org/.

Gray, Peter. *Free to Learn: Why Unleashing the Instinct to Play Will Make Our Children Happier, More Self-Reliant, and Better Students for Life*. Basic Books, 2013.

Historical Dictionary of Psychiatry. "Anhedonia." Accessed June 16, 2025. https://historical_psychiatry.en-academic.com/9/Anhedonia.

Johnson, Russell E., Stanley B. Silverman, Aarti Shyamsunder, et al. "Acting superior but actually inferior?: Correlates and consequences of workplace arrogance." *Human Performance* 23, No. 5 (2010): 403-427. https://doi.org/10.1080/08959285.2010.515279.

Joshanloo, Mohsen. "Fear and fragility of happiness as mediators of the relationship between insecure attachment and subjective well-being." *Personality and Individual Differences* (2018) https://doi.org/10.1016/j.paid.2017.11.016.

Joshanloo, M., et al. "Fragility of happiness beliefs across 15 national groups." *Journal of Happiness Studies* (July 2014) https://doi.org/10.1007/s10902-014-9553-0.

Jöstl, Gregor, Evelyn Bergsmann, Marko Lüftenegger, Barbara Schober, Christiane Spiel. "When will they blow my cover? The impostor phenomenon among Austrian doctoral students." *Zeitschrift für Psychologie* 220, No. 2 (2015): 109-120. https://doi.org/10.1027/2151-2604/a000102.

Kaiser Family Foundation. "Latest Federal Data Show That Young People Are More Likely Than Older Adults to Be Experiencing Symptoms of Anxiety or Depression." Updated March 2023. https://www.kff.org/mental-health/press-release/latest-federal-data-show-that-young-people-are-more-likely-than-older-adults-to-be-experiencing-symptoms-of-anxiety-or-depression/.

Kashdan, Todd B. *Curious? Discover the Missing Ingredient to a Fulfilling Life.* Harper Perennial, 2010.

Krznaric, Roman. *Carpe Diem Regained: The Vanishing Art of Seizing the Day.* Unbound, 2018.

Leary, Mark R. *The Curse of the Self: Self-Awareness, Egotism, and the Quality of Human Life.* Oxford University Press, 2007.

Leary, Mark R. "We can't all be right: Psychological and social implications of intellectual humility." Paper presented at the meeting of the Midwestern Psychological Association, Chicago (2018).

Li, Norman P., Mark van Vugt, Stephen M. Colarelli. "The Evolutionary Mismatch Hypothesis: Implications for Psychological Science." *Current Directions in Psychological Science 27, No. 1* (2017): 38-44. https://doi.org/10.1177/0963721417731378.

López-Muñoz, Francisco, Francisco Pérez-Fernández. "A History of the Alexithymia Concept and Its Explanatory Models: An Epistemological Perspective." *Frontiers in Psychiatry* (2020). PMID: 3208220. https://doi.org/10.3389/fpsyt.2019.01026.

Miyamoto,Yuri, Yukiko Uchida, Phoebe C. Ellsworth. "Culture and mixed emotions: Co-occurrence of positive and negative emotions in Japan and the United States." *Emotion 10, No 3* (2010): 404-15. https://doi.org/10.1037/a0018430

McMullen, M. N., K. D. Markman. "Downward counterfactuals and motivation: The wake-up call and the Pangloss effect." *Personality and Social Psychology Bulletin* (May 2000) https://journals.sagepub.com/doi/10.1177/0146167200267005.

Pychyl, Timothy. "Closing the Intention-Action Gap." Psychology Today (blog). 2009. https://www.psychologytoday.com/us/blog/dont-delay/200903/closing-the-intention-action-gap.

Roese, Neale, Mike Morrison. "The Psychology of Counterfactual Thinking." *Historical Social Research* (January 2009) https://www.researchgate.net/publication/255571704_The_Psychology_of_Counterfactual_Thinking.

Sakulku, Jaruwan, James Alexander. "The Impostor Phenomenon." *International Journal of Behavioral Science* 6, No. 1 (2011): 73-92. https://doi.org/10.14456/ijbs.2011.6.

Silverman, Stan B., Russell E. Johnson, Nicole McConnell, Alison Carr. "Arrogance: A Formula for Leadership Failure." *The Industrial-Organizational Psychologist* 50, No. 1 (2012): 21-28. http://homepages.se.edu/cvonbergen/files/2015/01/Arrogance_A-Formula-for-Leadership-Failure.pdf.

Steele, Eurídice Martínez, Barry M. Popkin, Boyd Swinburn, Carlos A. Monteiro. "The share of ultra-processed foods and the overall nutritional quality of diets in the US: evidence from a national representative cross-sectional study." *Population Health Metrics* 15, No. 1 (2017): PMID: 28193285. https://doi.org/10.1186/s12963-017-0119-3.

"Tom Hanks Says Self-Doubt Is 'A High-Wire Act That We All Walk.'" Fresh Air, NPR (August 2016). https://www.npr.org/2016/08/29/491800907/tom-hanks-says-self-doubt-is-a-high-wire-act-that-we-all-walk.

Wang, Hai-Jiang, Chang-Qin Lu, Oi-Ling Siu. "Job insecurity and job performance: The moderating role of organizational justice and the mediating role of work engagement." *Journal of Applied Psychology 100, No. 4* (2014): 1249-1258. https://doi.org/10.1037/a0038330.

Watson, Rebecca, Kate Harvey, Ciara McCabe, Shirley Reynolds. "Understanding anhedonia: a qualitative study exploring loss of interest and pleasure in adolescent depression." *European Child and Adolescent Psychiatry 29, No. 3* (2019): 489-499. https://doi.org/10.1007/s00787-019-01364-y.

Zhu, Meng, Yang Yang, Christopher K. Hsee. "The Mere Urgency Effect," *Journal of Consumer Research* 45, No. 3 (2018): 673-690. https://doi.org/10.1093/jcr/ucy008.

Chapter Five: Having a Resilient Growth Mindset

Boyce, W. Thomas. "Differential Susceptibility of the Developing Brain to Contextual Adversity and Stress." *Neuropsychopharmacology 41, No. 1* (2015): 142-62. https://doi.org/10.1038/npp.2015.294.

Burton, C. L., G. A. Bonanno. "Measuring Ability to Enhance and Suppress Emotional Expression: The Flexible Regulation of Emotional Expression (FREE) Scale." *Psychological Assessment* 28, No. 8 (2016): 929-941. https://doi.org/10.1037/pas0000231.

Chao, Melody Manchi, Sujata Visaria, Anirban Mukhopadhyay, Pajeev H. Dehejia. "Do rewards reinforce the growth mindset?: Joint effects of the growth mindset and incentive schemes in a field intervention." *Journal of Experimental Psychology: General* 46, No. 10 (2017): 1402-1419. https://doi.org/10.1037/xge0000355.

Colla, R., Paige Williams, Lindsay G. Oades, Jesus Camacho-Morles. "'A New Hope' for Positive Psychology: A Dynamic

Systems Reconceptualization of Hope Theory." *Frontiers in Psychology* 13 (2022) https://doi.org/10.3389/fpsyg.2022.809053.

Damisch, Lysann, Barbara Stoberock, Thomas Mussweiler. "Keep your fingers crossed!: How superstition improves performance." *Psychological Science* 21, No. 7 (2010): 1014-1020. https://doi.org/10.1177/0956797610372631.

Dunn, Barnaby, Leigh A. Burr, Harriet B. Smith, et al. "Turning gold into lead: Dampening appraisals reduce happiness and pleasantness and increase sadness during anticipation and recall of pleasant activities." *Behaviour Research and Therapy* 107 (2018): 19-33. https://doi.org/10.1016/j.brat.2018.05.003.

Frazier, Patricia, Howard Tennen, Margaret Gavian, Crystal Park, Patricia Tomich, Ty Tashiro. "Does Self-Reported Posttraumatic Growth Reflect Genuine Positive Change?" *Psychological Science* 20, No. 7 (2009): 912-919. https://doi.org/10.1111/j.1467-9280.2009.02381.x.

Gopnik, Alison. "Q & A: Alison Gopnik on babies and learning." UC Berkeley Research. https://vcresearch.berkeley.edu/news/qa-alison-gopnik-babies-and-learning.

Hayes, Steven, *Get Out of Your Mind and Into Your Life: The New Acceptance and Commitment Therapy*. New Harbinger, 2005.

Hayes, Steven C., Michael E. Levin, Jennifer Plumb-Vilardaga, Jennifer L. Villatte, Jacqueline Pisarello. "Acceptance and Commitment Therapy and Contextual Behavioral Science: Examining the Progress of a Distinctive Model of Behavioral and Cognitive Therapy." *Behavior Therapy Journal* 44, No. 2. (2011): 180-198. https://doi.org/10.1016/j.beth.2009.08.002.

Jäckel, Elisabeth, Alfred Zerres, Joachim Huffmeier. "Active Listening in Integrative Negotiation." *Communication Research* 0, No. 0 (2024) https://doi.org/10.1177/00936502241230711.

Levy-Gigi, Einat, Reut Donner, George A. Bonanno, G.A. "Free Your Mind: Emotional Expressive Flexibility Moderates the Effect of Stress on Post-Traumatic Stress Disorder Symptoms." *International Journal of Molecular Sciences 21, No. 15* (2020): 5355. https://doi.org/10.3390/ijms21155355.

Mancini, Anthony D., George A. Bonanno. "Predictors and parameters of resilience to loss: toward an individual differences model." *Journal of Personality* 77, No. 6 (2009): 1805-1832. https://doi.org/10.1111/j.1467-6494.2009.00601.x.

Mancini, A. D., Gabriele Prati, Sarah Black. "Self-worth mediates the effects of violent loss on PTSD symptoms." *Journal of Traumatic Stress 24, No. 1* (2011): 116-120. DOI: 10.1002/jts.20597.

Neenan, Michael. *Developing Resilience: A Cognitive-Behavioural Approach*. Routledge, 2018.

Pritchard, Duncan, Matthew Smith. "The psychology and philosophy of luck." New Ideas in Psychology 22, No. 1 (2004): 1-28.https://doi.org/10.1016/j.newideapsych.2004.03.001.

Rigney, Daniel. *The Matthew Effect: How Advantage Begets Further Advantage*. Columbia University Press, 2010.

Rozin, Paul, Edward B. Royzman. "Negativity Bias, Negativity Dominance, and Contagion." *Personality and Social Psychology Review* 5, Issue 4 (2001): 296-320. https://doi.org/10.1207/S15327957PSPR0504_2.

Snyder, C. R. *Handbook of Hope: Theory, Measures, and Applications*. Academic Press, 2000.

Söderkvist, Sven, Kajsa Ohlén, Ulf Dimberg. "How the Experience of Emotion is Modulated by Facial Feedback." *Journal of Nonverbal Behavior* 42 (2018): 129-151. https://doi.org/10.1007/s10919-017-0264-1.

Tedeschi, Richard, Lawrence Calhoun. "Posttraumatic Growth: Conceptual Foundations and Empirical Evidence." *Psychological Inquiry* 15, No. 1 (2004): 1-18. https://doi.org/10.1207/s15327965pli1501_01.

Werner, Emmy E., Ruth S. Smith. *Vulnerable, but Invincible:*

A Longitudinal Study of Resilient Children and Youth. McGraw-Hill, 1982.

Werner, E. E. "The Children of Kauai: Resiliency and recovery in adolescence and adulthood." Journal of Adolescent Health 13, No. 4 (1992): 262-268. https://doi.org/10.1016/1054-139X(92)90157-7.

Wiseman, Richard. The Luck Factor. Miramax, 2003.

Chapter Six: You Don't Have to Sit in Loneliness

Abbink, Klaus, Donna Harris. "In-group favouritism and out-group discrimination in naturally occurring groups." *PLoS One 14, No, 9.* (2019) e0221616. https://doi.org/10.1371/journal.pone.0221616.

American Psychological Association. "Stress in America 2020: A National Mental Health Crisis." Updated October 2020. https://www.apa.org/news/press/releases/stress/2020/report-october.

Association for Psychological Science. "Are People More Likely To Become Friends Based on Proximity Or Shared Values and Interests?." *ScienceDaily.* Accessed June 16, 2025. www.sciencedaily.com/releases/2008/06/080602163842.htm.

Back, Mitja D., Stefan C. Schmukle, Boris Egloff. "Becoming Friends by Chance" *Psychological Science 19, No. 5*

(2008): 439-440. https://doi.org/10.1111/j.1467-9280.2008.02106.x.

Billig, M., H. Tajfel. "Social categorization and similarity in intergroup behaviour." *European Journal of Social Psychology 3, No. 1 (1973): 27-52.* https://doi.org/10.1002/ejsp.2420030103.

Buechler, Jessica. "The Loneliness Epidemic Persists. A Post-Pandemic Look at the State of Loneliness among U.S. Adults." Cigna Health (2019) https://newsroom.thecignagroup.com/loneliness-epidemic-persists-post-pandemic-look.

Carter, C.S., et al. *Attachment and Bonding: A New Synthesis.* MIT Press, 2015.

Cohn, D., R. Morin. "Who Moves? Who Stays Put? Where's Home?" Pew Research (2008) https://www.pewresearch.org/social-trends/2008/12/17/who-moves-who-stays-put-wheres-home/.

Crooks, Valerie C., James Lubben, Diana B. Petitti, Deborah Little, Vicki Chiu. "Social Network, Cognitive Function, and Dementia Incidence Among Elderly Women." *Home American Journal of Public Health* 98, No. 7 (2008): 1221-1227. https://doi.org/10.2105/AJPH.2007.115923.

Cross, Alison. "'A concoction of disaster': Inside the CT post-win riot at UConn Storrs." *Hartford Courant* (2023) https:

//www.courant.com/2023/04/10/a-concoction-of-disaster-inside-the-post-win-riot-at-uconn-storrs/.

Dallago, Lorenza, Michael Lenzi, Douglas D. Perkins, Massimo Santinello. "Place Attachment in Adolescence." *Encyclopedia of Adolescence.* (2011): 2083-2091. https://doi.org/10.1007/978-1-4419-1695-2_403.

DePaulo, B. "If You Dine Alone, What Will People Think of You?" Psychology Today (blog). https://www.psychologytoday.com/us/blog/living-single/200804/if-you-dine-alone-what-will-people-think-you-part-1-see-if-you-can-predict.

Dewall, C. Nathan, Geoff Macdonald, Gregory D. Webster, et al. "Acetaminophen reduces social pain: behavioral and neural evidence." *Psychological Science* 21, No. 7 (2010): 931-937. https://doi.org/10.1177/0956797610374741.

Eisenberg, Marla E., Rachel E. Olson, Dianne Neumark-Sztainer, Mary Story, Linda H. Bearinger. "Correlations between family meals and psychosocial well-being among adolescents." *Archives of Pediatrics & Adolescent Medicine 158, No. 8* (2004): 792-796. https://doi.org/10.1001/archpedi.158.8.792.

Ertel, Karen, M. Gloria Glymour, Lisa F. Berkman. "Active Social Life May Delay Memory Loss Among US Elderly." *American Journal of Public Health* (2008) https://www.sciencedaily.com/releases/2008/05/080529162938.htm.

Fry, Richard. "Americans are moving at historically low rates, in part because Millennials are staying Put." Pew Research (2017) https://www.pewresearch.org/short-reads/2017/02/13/americans-are-moving-at-historically-low-rates-in-part-because-millennials-are-staying-put/.

Goldfarb, Anna. "How to Maintain Sibling Relationships," *New York Times* (May 8, 2018) https://www.nytimes.com/2018/05/08/smarter-living/how-to-maintain-sibling-relationships.html.

Hall, Jeffrey A. "How many hours does it take to make a friend?" *Journal of Social and Personal Relationships 36, No. 4 (2018): 1278-1296.* https://doi.org/10.1177/0265407518761225.

Harrison, Megan E., Mark L. Norris, Nicole Obeid, Meaghan Fu, Hannah Weinstangel, Margaret Sampson. "Systematic review of the effects of family meal frequency on psychosocial outcomes in youth." *Canadian Family Physician Journal* 61, No. 2 (2015): e96-e106. https://pmc.ncbi.nlm.nih.gov/articles/PMC4325878/.

Harvard Second Generation Study. "Grant Study of Adult Development." Accessed June 16, 2025. https://www.adult-developmentstudy.org/.

Hawkley, Louise C., Susanne Buecker, Till Kaiser, Maike Luhmann. "Loneliness from Young Adulthood to Old Age: Explaining Age Differences in Loneliness." *International*

Journal of Behavioral Development 46, No. 1 (2022): 39-49. https://doi.org/10.1177/0165025420971048.

Jensen, Melissa L., Francesca R. Dillman Carpentier, Camila Corvalán, et al. "Television viewing and using screens while eating: Associations with dietary intake in children and adolescents." *Appetite* 168:105670 (2022) https://doi.org/10.1016/j.appet.2021.105670.

Juhl, Jacob, Marios Biskas. "Nostalgia: An impactful social emotion." *Current Opinion in Psychology 49* (2023) https://doi.org/10.1016/j.copsyc.2022.101545.

Kluger, Jeffrey. *The Sibling Effect: What Bonds Among Brothers and Sisters Reveal About Us*. Riverhead, 2012.

LeRoy, Angie S., Kyle W. Murdock, Lisa M. Jaremka, Asad Loya, Chris P. Fagundes. "Cold Symptoms Feel Worse When People Feel Lonely." *APA* (2017) https://www.apa.org/news/press/releases/2017/03/cold-symptons.

LeRoy, A. S., et al. "Loneliness Predicts Self-Reported Cold Symptoms After a Viral Challenge." *Health Psychology* 36, No. 5 (2017): 512-520. https://doi.org/10.1037/hea0000467.

Morita, Ayako, TakehitoTakano, Keiko Nakamura, Masashi Kizuki, Kaoruko Seino. "Contribution of interaction with family, friends and neighbours, and sense of neighbourhood attachment to survival in senior citizens: 5-year follow-up study." *Social Science & Medicine* 70, No. 4 (2010): 543-549. https://doi.org/10.1016/j.socscimed.2009.10.057.

Newbury Massachusetts. "CDC: Alzehimers Disease and Healthy Aging CDC Loneliness and Social Isolation Linked to Serious Health Conditions." Accessed June 16, 2025. https://www.cityofnewburyport.com/health-department/bulletins/cdc-alzehimers-disease-and-healthy-aging-cdc-loneliness-and-social.

Perissinotto, Carla M., Irena Stijacic Cenzer, Kenneth H. E. Covinsky. "Loneliness in Older Persons: A Predictor of Functional Decline and Death." *Archives of Internal Medicine* 172, No. 14 (2012):1078-1083. https://doi.org/10.1001/archinternmed.2012.1993.

Peterson, Christopher, Martin Seligman. *Character Strengths and Virtues: A Handbook and Classification.* American Psychological Association / Oxford University Press, 2004.

Ratner, Rebecca K., Rebecca W. Hamilton. "Inhibited from Bowling Alone." Journal of Consumer Research 42, No. 2 (2015): 266-283. https://doi.org/10.1093/jcr/ucv012.

Rohrer, Julia, Tamás Keller, Felix Elwert. "Proximity can induce diverse friendships: A large randomized classroom experiment." *PLoS One* 16, No. 8 (2021): e0255097. https://doi.org/10.1371/journal.pone.0255097.

Scannell, Leila, Robert Gifford. "The experienced psychological benefits of place attachment." *Journal of Environmental Psychology* 51 (2017): 256-269. https://doi.org/10.1016/j.jenvp.2017.04.001.

Shandwick, Weber. "Civility in America 2018: Civility at Work and in Our Public Squares" (2018) https://webershandwick.com/news/civility-in-america-2018-civility-at-work-and-in-our-public-squares.

Slavich, George M., Grant S. Shields, Bailey D. Deal, Amy Gregory, Loren L. Toussant. "Alleviating Social Pain: A Double-Blind, Randomized, Placebo-Controlled Trial of Forgiveness and Acetaminophen." *Annals of Behavioral Medicine* 53, No. 12 (2019): 1045-1054. https://doi.org/10.1093/abm/kaz015.

Swann, W. B., Jr., M. Brooks. "Why Threats Trigger Compensatory Reactions: The Need for Coherence and Quest for Self-Verification." *Social Cognition* 30, No. 6 (2012): 758-777. https://doi.org/10.1521/soco.2012.30.6.758.

UNHCR: The UN Refugee Agency. "Number of refugees in the world: Global Trends Report." Updated June 2025. https://www.unhcr.org/us/global-trends.

Voorpostel, Marieke, Tanja van der Lippe, Henk Flap. "For better or worse: Negative life events and sibling relationships." *International Sociology* 27, No. 3 (2012): 330-348. https://doi.org/10.1177/0268580911423051.

Warnick, Melody. *This Is Where You Belong: The Art and Science of Loving the Place You Live.* Penguin, 2017.

Woolley, Michael E., Geoffrey L. Greif. "Measuring adult sibling communication comfort about sensitive issues." *Journal of Family Social Work* 23, No. 4: Siblings Across the Life Course (2020): 392-407. https://doi.org/10.1080/10522158.2020.1801550.

Woolley, M. E. *Adult Sibling Relationships.* Columbia University Press, 2015.

Yeung, Jerf W.K., Zhuoni Zhang, Tae Yeun Kim. "Volunteering and health benefits in general adults: cumulative effects and forms." *BMC Public Health* (2008) https://doi.org/10.1186/s12889-017-4561-8.

Zhang, Yun, Ginny Natale, Sean Clouston. "The Characteristics of Social Network Structure in Later Life in Relation to Incidence of Mild Cognitive Impairment and Conversion to Probable Dementia." *Journal of Alzheimer's Disease 81, No. 2* (2021): 699-710. https://doi.org/10.3233/JAD-201196.

Chapter Seven: The Mindful Relationship

Ahrons, Constance. *We're Still Family: What Grown Children Have to Say About Their Parents' Divorce.* Harper Perennial, 2005.

Averill, James R. "Studies on anger and aggression: Implications for theories of emotion." *American Psychologist* 38, No. 11 (1983): 1145-1160. https://doi.org/10.1037/0003-066X.38.11.1145.

Ben-Ze'ev, Aaron. *The Arc of Love: How Our Romantic Lives Change Over Time.* University of Chicago Press, 2019.

Daks, Jennifer S., Ronald D. Rogge. "Examining the correlates of psychological flexibility in romantic relationships and family dynamics: A meta-analysis." *Journal of Contextual Behavioral Science 18* (2020): 214-238. https://doi.org/10.1016/j.jcbs.2020.09.010.

Drigotas, Stephen M., Caryl E. Rusbult, Jennifer Weiselquist, Sarah W. Whitton. "Close Partner as Sculptor of the Ideal Self: Behavioral Affirmation and the Michelangelo Phenomenon." *Journal of Personality and Social Psychology* 77, No. 2 (1999): 293-323. https://doi.org/10.1037/0022-3514.77.2.293.

Haseltine, Eric. *Long Fuse, Big Bang: Achieving Long-Term Success through Daily Victories.* Hyperion, 2010.

Jäckel, Elisabeth, Alfred Zerres, Joachim Huffmeier. "Active Listening in Integrative Negotiation." *Communication Research* 0, No. 0 (2024) https://doi.org/10.1177/00936502241230711.

Nickerson, Raymond S. "Confirmation Bias: A Ubiquitous Phenomenon in Many Guises." *Review of General Psychology* 2, No. 2 (1998): 175-220. https://doi.org/10.1037/1089-2680.2.2.175.

Puett, Michael, Christine Gross-Loh. *The Path: A New Way to Think About Everything.* Viking Penguin, 2016.

Rogers, Shane L., Jill Howieson, Casey Neame. "I understand you feel that way, but I feel this way: The benefits of I-language and communicating perspective during conflict." *Peer Journal* (2018): 6:e4831. https://doi.org/10.7717/peerj.4831.

Schermerhorn, Alice C. "Associations of child emotion recognition with interparental conflict and shy child temperament traits." *Journal of Personal and Social Relationships* 36, No. 4 (2018): 1343-1366. https://doi.org/10.1177/0265407518762606.

Schermerhorn, A. C., John E. Bates, Aina Puce, Dennis L. Molfese. "Neurophysiological Correlates of Children's Processing of Interparental Conflict Cues." *Journal of Family Psychology* 29, No. 4 (2015): 518-527. https://doi.org/10.1037/fam0000088.

Waite, Linda J., Don Browning, William Doherty, Maggie Gallagher, Ye Luo, Scott M. Stanley. "Does Divorce Make People Happy? Findings from a Study of Unhappy Marriages." *Institute for American Values* (2002): 4-43.

https://www.researchgate.net/publication/237233376_Does_Divorce_Make_People_Happy_Findings_From_a_Study_of_Unhappy_Marriages.

Wang, Xiaoxia, Zhengzhi Feng. "A Narrative Review of Empirical Literature of Behavioral Activation Treatment for Depression." *Frontiers in Psychiatry* (2022): https://doi.org/10.3389/fpsyt.2022.845138.

Whitbourne, Susan Krauss. *The Search for Fulfillment: Revolutionary New Research That Reveals the Secret to Long-Term Happiness*. Ballantine, 2010.

Chapter Eight: Spirituality and Intuition Are Antidotes for Misery

Andrade, Chittaranjan, Rajiv Radhakrishnan. "Prayer and healing: A medical and scientific perspective on randomized controlled trials." *Indian Journal of Psychiatry* 51, No. 4 (2009): 247-253. https://doi.org/10.4103/0019-5545.58288.

Barber, Nigel. "A Cross-National Test of the Uncertainty Hypothesis of Religious Belief." *Cross-Cultural Research* 45, No. 3 (2011): 318-333. https://doi.org/10.1177/1069397111402465.

Benson, Herbert, John W. Lehmann, M.S. Malhotra, Ralph F. Goldman, Jeffrey Hopkins, Mark D. Epstein. "Body temperature changes during the practice of Tum-mo yoga." *Nature* 295 (1982): 234-236. https://doi.org/10.1038/295234a0.

Bower, Julienne E., Michael R. Irwin. "Mind-body therapies and control of inflammatory biology: A descriptive review." *Brain, Behavior, and Immunity* 51 (2016): 1-11. https://doi.org/10.1016/j.bbi.2015.06.012.

Bremner, R. H., S. L. Koole, B. J. Bushman. "'Pray for those who mistreat you': Effects of prayer on anger and aggression." *Personality and Social Psychology Bulletin* 37, No. 6 (2011): 830-837: https://doi.org/10.1177/0146167211402215.

Byrd, Cathy. *The Boy Who Knew Too Much: An Astounding True Story of a Young Boy's Past-Life Memories.* Hay House, 2017.

Cotton, Sian, Jerren C. Weekes, Meghan E. McGrady. "Spirituality and religiosity in urban adolescents with asthma." *Journal of Religion and Health 51, No. 1 (2013): 118-131.* https://doi.org/10.1007/s10943-010-9408-x.

Dosa, David M. "A Day in the Life of Oscar the Cat." *The New England Journal of Medicine* 357, No. 4 (2007): 328-329. https://doi.org/10.1056/NEJMp078108.

Erlandsson, Kerstin, Helen Lindgren, Anna Davidson-Bremborg, Ingela Rådestad. "Women's premonitions prior to the death of their baby in utero and how they deal with feeling that their baby may be unwell." *Acta Obstetricia et*

Gynecologica Scandinavica 91, No. 1 (2012): 28-33. https://doi.org/10.1111/j.1600-0412.2011.01209.x.

Galen, Luke W., James D. Kloet. "Mental well-being in the religious and the non-religious: Evidence for a curvilinear relationship." *Mental Health, Religion, and Culture* 7 (2011): 673-689. https://doi.org/10.1080/13674676.2010.510829.

Haddow, Gill. *Embodiment and everyday cyborgs: Technologies that alter subjectivity*. Manchester University Press, 2021.

Hutson, Matthew. *The 7 Laws of Magical Thinking: How Irrational Beliefs Keep Us Happy, Healthy, and Sane*. Plume, 2013.

Jamil, Aneeque, Sai Dheerjah Gutlapalli, Marya Ali. "Meditation and Its Mental and Physical Health Benefits in 2023." *Cureus 15, No. 6* (2023): e40650. https://doi.org/10.7759/cureus.40650.

Kapalle, Praveen K., Hannu Kuusela, Donald R. Lehmann. "The role of intuition in CEO acquisition decisions." *Journal of Business Research* 167, No. 3 (2023) 114139. https://doi.org/10.1016/j.jbusres.2023.114139.

Moreno, Juan J. "Modulation of inflammatory response and pain by mind-body therapies as Meditation." *Brain Behavior and Immunity Integrative* 5 (2024): https://doi.org/10.1016/j.bbii.2023.100036.

Navarro, Joe, Marvin Karlins. *What Every Body Is Saying: An Ex-FBI Agent's Guide to Speed-Reading People.* William Morrow Paperbacks, 2008.

Newberg, Andrew, Mark Robert Waldman. *How God Changes Your Brain: Breakthrough Findings from a Leading Neuroscientist.* Ballantine Books, 2010.

Newberg, A., M. R. Waldman. *How Enlightenment Changes Your Brain: The New Science of Transformation.* Avery, 2016.

Peñacoba-Puente, Cecilia, Francisco Javier Carmona Monge, Dolores Marín Morales. "Pregnancy worries: A longitudinal study of Spanish women." *Journal Acta Obstetricia et Gynecologica Scandinavica* 90, No. 9 (2011): 1030-1035. https://doi.org/10.1111/j.1600-0412.2011.01208.x.

Shroder, Tom. *Old Souls: Compelling Evidence from Children Who Remember Past Lives.* Simon & Schuster, 2011.

Stevenson, Ian. *Children Who Remember Previous Lives: A Question of Reincarnation.* University of Virginia Press, 1988.

Sylvia, Claire, Willaim Novak. *A Change of Heart: A Memoir.* Grand Central, 1998.

Verny, Thomas. *The Embodied Mind: Understanding the Mysteries of Cellular Memory, Consciousness, and Our Bodies.* Pegasus, 2023.

Chapter Nine: Be True and Genuine With Positivity

Andriote, John-Manuel. *Victory Deferred: How AIDS Changed Gay Life in America.* University of Chicago Press, 1999.

Andriote, J. M. *Stonewall Strong: Gay Men's Heroic Fight for Resilience, Good Health, and a Strong Community.* Rowman and Littlefield, 2017.

Bernhard, Toni. *How to Live Well with Chronic Pain and Illness: A Mindful Guide.* Wisdom Books, 2015.

Bernhard, T. *How to Be Sick: A Buddhist-Inspired Guide for the Chronically Ill and Their Caregivers.* Wisdom Books, 2018.

Brown, Brené. *Daring Greatly: How the Courage to Be Vulnerable Transforms the Way We Live, Love, Parent, and Lead.* Avery, 2015.

Flanagan, Róisín M., Jennifer E. Symonds. "Children's self-talk in naturalistic classroom settings in middle childhood: A systematic literature review." *Educational Research Review* 35, No. 3 (February 2022) https://doi.org/10.1016/j.edurev.2022.100432.

Gross-Loh, C., M. Puett. *The Path: A New Way to Think About Everything.* Penguin Viking, 2016.

Hayes, Steven C., Michael E. Levin, Jennifer Plumb-Vilardaga, Jennifer L. Villatte, Jacqueline Pistorello. "Acceptance and

Commitment Therapy and Contextual Behavioral Science: Examining the Progress of a Distinctive Model of Behavioral and Cognitive Therapy." *Behavior Therapy Journal* 44, No. 2 (2011): 180-198. https://doi.org/10.1016/j.beth.2009.08.002.

Hurlburt, Russell T., Christopher L. Heavey, Jason M. Kelsey. "Toward a Phenomenology of Inner Speaking." *Consciousness and Cognition* 22, No 4 (2013): 1477-1494. https://doi.org/10.1016/j.concog.2013.10.003.

Joseph, Stephen. *Authentic: How to Be Yourself and Why It Matters.* Little Brown and Co, 2017.

Lowry, C.A., J.H. Hollis, A. de Vries. "Identification of an immune-responsive mesolimbocortical serotonergic system: Potential role in regulation of emotional behavior." *Neuroscience* 146, No. 2 (2007): 756-772. https://doi.org/10.1016/j.neuroscience.2007.01.067.

Oleś, Piotr K., Thomas M. Brinthaupt, Rachel Dier, Dominika Polak. "Types of Inner Dialogues and Functions of Self-Talk: Comparisons and Implications." *Frontiers in Psychology* 11 (March 2020) https://doi.org/10.3389/fpsyg.2020.00227.

Rogers, Carl. *On Becoming a Person: A Therapist's View of Psychotherapy.* Houghton Mifflin, 1961.

Schweer-Collins, Maria L., Brianna Mintz, Elizabeth A. Skowron. "Differentiation of Self in Bowen Family Systems

Theory," *Encyclopedia of Couple and Family Therapy* (2017) https://link.springer.com/referenceworkentry/10.1007/978-3-319-15877-8_345-1.

Titelman, Peter, ed. *Differentiation of Self: Bowen Family System Theory Perspectives.* Routledge, 2015.

White, M. D. *The Decline of the Individual.* Palgrave Macmillan, 2017.

Chapter Ten: We Need Validation

Albers, Susan. "You're the Star of the Show With Main Character Syndrome." Cleveland Clinic (December 15, 2023) https://health.clevelandclinic.org/what-to-know-about-main-character-syndrome.

Baumeister, Roy F., Lauren E. Brewer, Dianne M. Tice, Jean M. Twenge. "Thwarting the Need to Belong: Understanding the Interpersonal and Inner Effects of Social Exclusion." *Social and Personality Psychology Compass* 1, No. 1 (2007): 506-520. https://doi.org/10.1111/j.1751-9004.2007.00020.x.

Brooks, David. *The Road to Character.* Random House, 2016.

Brown, Brené. *Daring Greatly: How the Courage to Be Vulnerable Transforms the Way We Live, Love, Parent, and Lead.* Avery, 2015.

Cattell, Raymond B. *Personality and mood by questionnaire (The*

Jossey-Bass behavioral science series) Jossey-Bass Publishers, 1973.

Chopik, William J., Ed O'Brien, Sara Konrath. "Differences in Empathic Concern and Perspective Taking Across 63 Countries." *Journal of Cross-Cultural Psychology* 48, No. 1 (2016): 23-38. https://doi.org/10.1177/0022022116673910.

Deri, Sebastian, Shai Davidai, Thomas Gilovich. "Home alone: Why people believe others' social lives are richer than their own." *Journal of Personality and Social Psychology* 46, No. 1 (2017): 858-877. https://doi.org/10.1037/pspa0000105.

Emmons, Robert A. *Gratitude Works!: A 21-Day Program for Creating Emotional Prosperity.* Jossey-Bass, 2013.

Fritz, Megan M., Christina N. Armenta, Lisa C. Walsh. "Gratitude facilitates healthy eating behavior in adolescents and young adults." *Journal of Experimental Social Psychology* 81 (2019): 4-14. https://doi.org/10.1016/j.jesp.2018.08.011.

Gilovich, Thomas. *How We Know What Isn't So: The Fallibility of Human Reason in Everyday Life.* Free Press, 2008.

Hamamura, Takeshi, Yi Xu. "Changes in Chinese culture as examined through changes in personal pronoun usage." *Journal of Cross-Cultural Psychology 46, No. 7* (2015): 930-941. https://doi.org/10.1177/0022022115592968.

Jans-Beken, Lilian, Nele Jacobs, Mayke Janssens. "Gratitude and health: An updated review," *The Journal of Positive Psychology* (2019): 743-782. https://doi.org/10.1080/17439760.2019.1651888.

Karpman, Stephen B. *A Game Free Life. The definitive book on the Drama Triangle and Compassion Triangle by the originator and author.* Drama Triangle, 2014.

Kaufman, Scott B. *Transcend: The New Science of Self-Actualization.* TarcherPerigee, 2020.

Kaufman, Scott B., David B. Yaden, Elizabeth Hyde, Eli Tsukayama. "The Light vs. Dark Triad of Personality: Contrasting Two Very Different Profiles of Human Nature." *Frontiers in Psychology 10* (2019) https://doi.org/10.3389/fpsyg.2019.00467.

Konrath, Sara, Femida Handy. "The Development and Validation of the Motives to Donate Scale." *Nonprofit and Voluntary Sector Quarterly* 47, No. 2 (2017): 347-375. https://doi.org/10.1177/0899764017744894.

Leary, Mark R., Kate J. Diebels, Erin K. Davisson. "Cognitive and Interpersonal Features of Intellectual Humility." *Personality and Social Psychology Bulletin 43, No. 6* (2017): 793-813. https://doi.org/10.1177/0146167217697695.

Lee, Kibeom, Michael Ashton. *The H-Factor of Personality: Why Some People are Manipulative, Self-Entitled, Materialistic, and Exploitive—And Why It Matters for Everyone.* Wilfrid Laurier University Press, 2012.

Paulhus, D., K. M. Williams. "The Dark Triad of Personality: Narcissism, Machiavellianism, and Psychopathy." *Journal of Research in Personality 36, No. 6* (2002): 556-563. https://doi.org/10.1016/S0092-6566(02)00505-6.

Rowland, Lee, Oliver Scott Curry. "A range of kindness activities boosts happiness." *The Journal of Social Psychology* 159, No. 3 (2019): 340-343. https://doi.org/10.1080/00224545.2018.1469461.

Twenge, Jean M. *Generation Me: Why Today's Young Americans Are More Confident, Assertive, Entitled—and More Miserable Than Ever Before.* Atria, 2014.

White, Lawrence T. *Culture Conscious: Briefings on Culture, Cognition, and Behavior.* Wiley, 2020.

Wong, Y. Joel, Jesse Owen, Nicole T. Gabana, et al. "Does gratitude writing improve the mental health of psychotherapy clients? Evidence from a randomized controlled trial." *Psychotherapy Research 28, No. 2 (2018): 192-202.* https://doi.org/10.1080/10503307.2016.1169332.

Yang, Man, Hao Wang, Jun Yao. "Relationship between Intergenerational Emotional Support and Subjective Well-Being among Elderly Migrants in China: The mediating role of loneliness and self-esteem." *International Journal of Environmental Research and Public Health 19, No. 21 (2022): 14567.* https://doi.org/10.3390/ijerph192114567.

Chapter Eleven: The Body Knows What It Needs

Ali, Fatma Romeh M., Israel T. Agaku, Saida R. Sharapova, Elizabeth A. Reimels, David M. Homa. "Onset of Regular Smoking Before Age 21 and Subsequent Nicotine Dependence and Cessation Behavior Among US Adult Smokers." *Public Health Research, CDC* 17 (2020): E06. https://doi.org/10.5888/pcd17.190176.

Buysse, Daniel J. "Sleep Health: Can We Define It? Does It Matter?" *Sleep* 37, No. 1 (2014): 9-17. https://doi.org/10.5665/sleep.3298.

Carabotti, Marilla, Annunziata Scirocco, Maria Antoinetta Maselli, Carola Severi. "The gut-brain axis: Interactions between enteric microbiota, central and enteric nervous systems." *Annals of Gastroenterology* 28, No. 2 (2015): 203-209. https://pmc.ncbi.nlm.nih.gov/articles/PMC4367209/.

Centers for Disease Control and Prevention. "Alcohol Use and Your Health." Accessed June 16, 2025. https://www.cdc.gov/alcohol/about-alcohol-use/index.html.

Centers for Disease Control and Prevention: National Center for Health Statistics. "NCHS: Data Briefs." Accessed June 16, 2025. https://www.cdc.gov/nchs/products/databriefs.htm.

Cherkas, Lynn F., Janice L. Hunkin, Bernet S. Kato, et al. "The Association Between Physical Activity in Leisure Time and Leukocyte Telomere Length." *Archives of Internal Medicine* 168, No. 2 (2008): 154-158. https://doi.org/10.1001/archinternmed.2007.39.

Choi, Karmel W., Chia-Yen Chen, Murray B. Stein. "Assessment of Bidirectional Relationships Between Physical Activity and Depression Among Adults: A 2-Sample Mendelian Randomization Study." *JAMA Psychiatry* 76, No. 4 (2019): 399-408. https://doi.org/10.1001/jamapsychiatry.2018.4175.

Chong, Yinong, Cheryl D. Fryer, Quiping Gu. "Prescription Sleep Aid Use Among Adults: United States, 2005-2010." *NCHS Data Brief* No. 127. CDC (2013): 1-8. https://www.cdc.gov/nchs/products/databriefs/db127.htm.

Curley, Bob. "Smoking damages chromosomes and causes premature aging, study finds." *Medical News Today* (September 16, 2023). https://www.medicalnewstoday.com/articles/smoking-can-cause-chromosome-damage-and-lead-to-quicker-aging-study-reports.

Gibbons, Travis D., James D. Cotter, Philip N. Ainslie, et al. "Fasting for 20 hours does not affect exercise-induced increases in circulating BDNF in humans." *The Journal of Physiology* 601, No. 11 (2023): 2121-2137. https://doi.org/10.1113/JP283582.

Griffin, Éadaoin W., Sinéad Mullally, Carole Foley, Stuart A. Warmington, Shane M. O'Mara, Aine M. Kelly. "Aerobic exercise improves hippocampal function and increases BDNF in the serum of young adult males." *Physiology and Behavior* 104, No. 5 (2011): 934-941. https://doi.org/10.1016/j.physbeh.2011.06.005.

Jerath, Ravinder, Molly W. Crawford, Vernon A. Barnes, Kyler Harden. "Self-Regulation of Breathing as a Primary Treatment for Anxiety." *Applied Psychophysiology and Biofeedback* 40, No. 2 (2015): 107-115. https://doi.org/10.1007/s10484-015-9279-8.

Li, Yanping, An Pan, Dong D. Wang, et al. "Impact of Healthy Lifestyle Factors on Life Expectancies in the US Population." *Circulation* 138, No. 4 (2018): 345-355. https://doi.org/10.1161/CIRCULATIONAHA.117.032047.

National Heart, Lung, and Blood Institute. "Heart-Healthy Living: Aim for a Healthy Weight."

Updated March 2022. https://www.nhlbi.nih.gov/health/heart-healthy-living/healthy-weight.

National Institutes of Health. "Physical Wellness Toolkit." Updated January 2025.

https://www.nih.gov/health-information/your-healthiest-self-wellness-toolkits/physical-wellness-toolkit..

Nyer, Maren B., Lindsey B. Hopkins, Megha Nagaswami. "A Randomized Controlled Trial of Community-Delivered Heated Hatha Yoga for Moderate-to-Severe Depression." *Journal of Clinical Psychiatry* 84, No. 6 (2023) https://doi.org/10.4088/JCP.22m14621.

Porges, Stephen W. *The Polyvagal Theory: Neurophysiological Foundations of Emotions, Attachment, Communication, and Self-Regulation*. W. W. Norton & Company, 2011.

Rahmati, Masoud, San Lee, Dong Keon Yon. "Physical activity and prevention of mental health complications: An umbrella review." *Neuroscience & Biobehavioral Reviews* (2024) https://doi.org/10.1016/j.neubiorev.2024.105641.

Riegel, Barbara, Sandra Dunbar, Donna Fitzsimmons, et al. "Self-care research: Where are we now? Where are we going?" *International Journal of Nursing Studies* 116 (2021): 103402. https://doi.org/10.1016/j.ijnurstu.2019.103402.

Soga, Masashi, Kevin J. Gaston, Yuichi Yamura. "Gardening is beneficial for health: A meta-analysis." *Preventive Medicine Reports* 5 (2017): 92-99. DOI: 10.1016/j.pmedr.2016.11.007.

Summer, Jay Vera, Abhinav Singh. "Sleep Deprivation: Symptoms, Treatments, and Effects." Sleep Foundation. (2025) https://www.sleepfoundation.org/sleep-deprivation.

Yoshimura, Reiji, Atsuko Ikenouchi-Sugita, Hikaru Hori, et al. "Blood levels of brain-derived neurotrophic factor (BDNF) in major depressive disorder." *Seishin Shinkeigaku Zasshi Journal* 112, No. 10 (2010): 982-985.

Chapter Twelve: Happiness Means Being Here Right Now

Abramowitz, Jonathan S., Michael G. Wheaton, Eric A. Storch. "The status of hoarding as a symptom of obsessive-compulsive disorder." *Behaviour Research and Therapy* 46, No. 9 (2008): 1026-1033. https://doi.org/10.1016/j.brat.2008.05.006.

Atchley, Paul, Amelia C. Warden. "The need of young adults to text now: Using delay discounting to assess informational choice." *Journal of Applied Research in Memory and Cognition* 1, No. 4 (2012): 229-234. https://doi.org/10.1016/j.jarmac.2012.09.001.

Ayers, Catherine R., Sanjaya Saxena, Shahrokh Golshan, Julie Loebach Wetherell. "Age at onset and clinical features of late life compulsive hoarding." *International Journal of Geriatric Psychiatry* 25, No. 2 (2010): 142-149. https://doi.org/10.1002/gps.2310.

Bai, Yang, Joseph Ocampo, Gening Jin, et al. "Awe, daily stress, and elevated life satisfaction," *Journal of Personality and Social Psychology* 120, No. 4 (2021): 837-860. https://doi.org/10.1037/pspa0000267.

Barton, Jo, Jules Pretty. "What is the Best Dose of Nature and Green Exercise for Improving Mental Health? A Multi-Study Analysis." *Environmental Science and Technology* 44, No. 10 (2010): 3947-3955. https://doi.org/10.1021/es903183r.

Bellezza, Silvia, Neeru Paharia, Anat Keinan. "Research: Why Americans Are So Impressed by Busyness." *Harvard Business Review* (December 15, 2016) https://hbr.org/2016/12/research-why-americans-are-so-impressed-by-busyness.

Bratman, Gregory N., J. Paul Hamilton, Kevin S. Hahn, Gretchen C. Daily, James J. Gross. "Nature experience reduces rumination and subgenual prefrontal cortex activation." *Proceedings of the National Academy of Sciences* 112, No. 28 (2015): 8567-8572. https://doi.org/10.1073/pnas.1510459112.

Chen, Chun-Chu, James F. Petrick. "Health and Wellness Benefits of Travel Experiences: A Literature Review." *Journal of Travel Research* 52, No. 6 (2013): 709-719. https://doi.org/10.1177/0047287513496477.

"Clean homes and children's well-being." American Economic Association meeting, and the Panel Study of Income Dynamics.

Clingingsmith, David. "Negative Emotions, Income, and Welfare: Causal Estimates from the PSID." *Journal of Economic Behavior and Organization* 130 (2016): 1-19. https://doi.org/10.1016/j.jebo.2016.07.004.

Csikszentmihalyi, Mihaly. *Flow: The Psychology of Optimal Experience.* Harper Perennial, 2008.

Dunifon, R. "Clean homes can boost children's adult education and earnings," American Economic Association Meeting, University of Michigan (March 2001) http://www.ns.umich.edu/new/releases/3865-clean-homes-can-boost-children-s-adult-education-and-earnings.

Dunn, Elizabeth. Michael Norton. *Happy Money: The Science of Happier Spending.* Simon and Schuster, 2014.

Frank, Robert H. *The Darwin Economy: Liberty, Competition, and the Common Good.* Princeton University Press, 2011.

Feldman, David B., Diane E. Dreher. "Can Hope Be Changed in 90 Minutes? Testing the Efficacy of a Single-Session Goal-Pursuit Intervention for College Students." *Journal of Happiness Studies* 13 (2011): 745-759. https://doi.org/10.1007/s10902-011-9292-4.

Frost, Randy O., Meredith S. Krause, Gail Steketee. "Hoarding and Obsessive-Compulsive Symptoms." *Behavior Modifiation* 20, No. 1 (1996) https://doi.org/10.1177/01454455960201006.

Gaspar, John M., Gregory J. Christie, David J. Prime, Pierre Jolicoeur, John J. McDonald. "Inability to suppress salient distractors predicts low visual working memory capacity." *Proceedings of the National Academy of Sciences*

113, No. 13 (2016): 3693-3698. https://doi.org/10.1073/pnas.1523471113.

Han, Ke-Tsung, Li-Wen Ruan, Li-Shih Liao. "Effects of Indoor Plants on Human Functions: A Systematic Review with Meta-Analyses." *International Journal of Environmental Research and Public Health* 19, No. 12 (2022): 7454. https://doi.org/10.3390/ijerph19127454.

Hershfield, Hal E., Cassie Mogilner, Uri Barnea. "People Who Choose Time Over Money Are Happier." *Social Psychological and Personality Science* (2016): 1-10. https://doi.org/10.1177/1948550616649239.

Horowitz, Juliana Menasce, Kim Parker. "How Americans View Their Jobs." Pew Research Center (March 30, 2023) https://www.pewresearch.org/wp-content/uploads/sites/20/2023/03/ST_2023.03.30_Culture-of-Work_Report.pdf.

Holzman, David C. "What's in a Color? The Unique Human Health Effects of Blue Light." *Environmental Health Perspectives* 118, NO. 1 (2010): A22-A27. https://doi.org/10.1289/ehp.118-a22.

Hornsey, Matthew J., Paul G. Bain, Emily A. Harris, et al. "How Much Is Enough in a Perfect World? Cultural Variation in Ideal Levels of Happiness, Pleasure, Freedom, Health, Self-Esteem, Longevity, and Intelligence."

Psychological Science 29, No. 9 (2018): 1393-1404. https://doi.org/10.1177/0956797618768058.

Hruska, Bryce, Sarah D. Pressman, Kestutis Bendinskas, Brooks B. Gump. "Vacation frequency is associated with metabolic syndrome and symptoms." *Psychology & Health* 35, No. 1. (2019): 1-15. https://doi.org/10.1080/08870446.2019.1628962.

Hunt, Melissa G., Rachel Marx, Courtney Lipson, Jordyn Young. "No More FOMO: Limiting Social Media Decreases Loneliness and Depression." *Journal of Social and Clinical Psychology* 37, No. 10 (2018): 751-768. https://doi.org/10.1521/jscp.2018.37.10.751.

Ideno, Y., K. Hayashi, et al. "Blood pressure-lowering effect of Shinrin-yoku (forest bathing): a systematic review and meta-analysis." *MC in Complementary and Alternative Medicine* 17, No. 1 (2017): 409. https://doi.org/10.1186/s12906-017-1912-z.

"Injury Control: Transportation Safety: Distracted Driving," CDC https://www.cdc.gov/transportationsafety/distracted_driving/.

Jamea, Emily N., Leah A. McCaskill, Rachel B. Needle. "Sexual Satisfaction: Exploring the Role of Flow." *Journal of Sex & Marital Therapy 47, No. 5* (2021): 481-491. https://doi.org/10.1080/0092623X.2021.1898503.

Kahneman, Daniel, Angus Deaton. "High income improves evaluation of life but not emotional well-being." *Proceedings of the National Academy of Sciences* 107, No 38 (2010): 16489-16493. https://doi.org/10.1073/pnas.1011492107.

Kitchin, John. *Slomo and the New World*. Amiford Publishing, 2005.

Klepeis, Neil E., William C. Nelson, Wayne R. Ott, et al. "The National Human Activity Pattern Survey (NHAPS): A resource for assessing exposure to environmental pollutants." *Journal of Exposure Science and Environmental Epidemiology* 11 (2001): 231-252. https://www.nature.com/articles/7500165.

Konok, Veronika, Dóra Gigler, Boróka Mária Bereczky, Adam Miklosi. "Humans' attachment to their mobile phones and its relationship with interpersonal attachment style." *Computers in Human Behavior* 61, No. 3 (2016): 537-547. https://doi.org/10.1016/j.chb.2016.03.062.

Lambert, Kelly. *Lifting Depression: A Neuroscientist's Hands-On Approach to Activating Your Brain's Healing Power*. Basic Books, 2008.

Louv, Richard. *The Nature Principle: Reconnecting with Life in a Virtual Age*. Algonquin Books, 2012.

Magnusson, Margareta. *The Gentle Art of Swedish Death*

Cleaning: How to Free Yourself and Your Family from a Lifetime of Clutter. Scribner, 2018.

Milyavskaya, Marina, Mark Saffran, Nora Hope, Richard Koestner. "Fear of Missing Out: Prevalence, Dynamics, and Consequences of Experiencing FOMO." *Motivation and Emotion* 42 (2018): 725-737. https://doi.org/10.1007/s11031-018-9683-5.

Nieuwenhuis, Marlon, Craig Knight, Tom Postmes, S. Alexander Haslam. "The Relative Benefits of Green Versus Lean Office Space: Three Field Experiments," *Journal of Experimental Psychology Applied* 20, No. 3 (2014): 199-214. https://doi.org/10.1037/xap0000024.

Oxford Reference. The Goldilocks Effect. Accessed June 16, 2025. https://www.oxfordreference.com/display/10.1093/oi/authority.20110803095858415.

Pang, Alex Soojung-Kim. *Rest: Why You Get More Done When You Work Less.* Basic Books, 2016.

Park, Bum Jin, Yuko Tsunetsugu, Tamami Kasetani, Takahide Kagawa, Yoshifumi Miyazaki. "The physiological effects of Shinrin-yoku (taking in the forest atmosphere or forest bathing) experiments in 24 forests across Japan." *Environmental Health and Preventive Medicine 15, No. 1* (2009): 18-26. https://doi.org/10.1007/s12199-009-0086-9.

Pennebaker, James W. *Opening Up: The Healing Power of Expressing Emotions.* The Guilford Press, 1997.

Pertusa, Alberto, Randy O. Frost, David Mataix-Cols. "When hoarding is a symptom of OCD: A case series and implications for DSM-V." *Behavior Research and Therapy* 48, No. 10 (2010): 1012-1020. https://doi.org/10.1016/j.brat.2010.07.003.

Rogers, Kara. "Biophilia hypothesis (Erich Fromm)." *Britannica.* https://www.britannica.com/science/biophilia-hypothesis.

Roster, Catherine A., Joseph R. Ferrari, M. Peter Jurkat. "The dark side of home: Assessing possession 'clutter' on subjective well-being." *Journal of Environmental Psychology* 46 (2016): 132-141. https://doi.org/10.1016/j.jenvp.2016.03.003.

Safron, Adam. "What is orgasm? A model of sexual trance and climax via rhythmic entrainment." *Socioaffective Neuroscience and Psychology* 6 (2016) doi: 10.3402/snp.v6.31763.

Southey, Robert. *Goldilocks and the Three Bears* (1837).

"State of the American Vacation: Project Time Off." US Travel Association (2018) https://www.ustravel.org/system/files/media_root/document/StateofAmericanVacation2018.pdf.

Steketee, Gail, Randy Frost. *Stuff: Compulsive Hoarding and the Meaning of Things.* Mariner, 2011.

Sudimac, Sonja. Vera Sale, Simone Kühn. "How nature nurtures: Amygdala activity decreases as the result of a one-hour walk in nature." *Molecular Psychiatry* 27, No. 11 (2022): 1-7. https://doi.org/10.1038/s41380-022-01720-6.

"The Monitor of Engagement with the Natural Environment Survey." United Kingdom (August 2014) https://www.gov.uk/government/collections/monitor-of-engagement-with-the-natural-environment-survey-purpose-and-results.

Vartanian, Lenny R., Kristin M. Kernan, Brian Wansink. "Clutter, chaos, and overconsumption: The role of mindset in stressful and chaotic food environments," *Environment and Behavior* 49, No. 2 (2017): 215-223. https://doi.org/10.1177/0013916516628178.

Watson, Jason M., David L. Strayer. "Supertaskers: Profiles in Extraordinary Multitasking Ability." *Psychonomic Bulletin & Review* 17 (2010): 479-485. https://doi.org/10.3758/PBR.17.4.479.

Weinstein, Netta, Andrew K. Przybylski, Richard M. Ryan. "Can Nature Make Us More Caring? Effects of Immersion in Nature on Intrinsic Aspirations and Generosity." *Personality and Social Psychology Bulletin* 35, No. 10 (2009): 1315-1329. https://doi.org/10.1177/0146167209341649.

White, Mathew P., Ian Alcock, James Grellier, et al. "Spending at least 120 minutes a week in nature is associated with good health and well-being." *Scientific Reports* 9 (2019): 7730. https://doi.org/10.1038/s41598-019-44097-3.

Wilson, E.O. *Biophilia*. Harvard University Press, 1984.

Chapter Thirteen: What Do We Value?

Cerfolio, Nina E. *Psychoanalytic and Spiritual Perspectives on Terrorism: Desire for Destruction. Routledge,* 2024.

Hayes, Steven. *Get Out of Your Mind and Into Your Life: The New Acceptance and Commitment Therapy.* New Harbinger, 2005.

Ji, L. L., J. R. Dickman, et al. "Exercise-Induced Hormesis May Help Healthy Aging." *Dose-Response* (January 2010) https://doi.org/10.2203/dose-response.09-048.Ji.

"Mental health threats during the COVID-19 pandemic." CDC (2022) cdc.gov/media/releases/2022/p0331-youth-mental-health-covid-19.html.

Philosophy 312: Oriental Philosophy, Main Concepts of Confucianism. Lander University. http://philosophy.lander.edu/oriental/main.html.

Pillemer, Karl. *30 Lessons for Living: Tried and True Advice from the Wisest Americans*. Avery Books, 2012.

Rokeach, Milton. *The Nature of Human Values.* The Free Press, 1973.

Shweder, Richard A., editor. *Welcome to Middle Age! (And Other Cultural Fictions).* The John D. and Catherine T. MacArthur Foundation Series on Mental Health and Development. The University of Chicago Press, 1998.